ASTRAL PROJECTION

This book is a complete and straightforward guide to Astral Projection, that age-old technique of *out-of-the-body experience* which is a natural faculty of the human psyche.

Written in a flowing and easily-readable style, this book carries the student gently, yet thoroughly, through the essential stages of inner growth and development of psychic potential necessary to the achievement of Astral Projection in full consciousness.

Not only are the requisite practices set forth in a detailed and lucid manner, but the vital reasons for undertaking them are made plain. Furthermore, the authors demonstrate the great benefit to be derived from the various practices in themselves.

From the first simple steps such as breathing exercises, through to the splendor of conscious adventure in the astral worlds, this book is replete with valuable information and sensitive guidance.

For all who have wished for a sane, in-depth and honest approach to *out-of-the-body experience*, this book will be a vital addition to its subject.

D0049987

The Llewellyn Practical Guides to Personal Power

To some people, the idea that "magick" is *practical* comes as a surprise. It shouldn't!

The entire basis for what we call "magick" is to exercise influence over one's personal world in order to satisfy our needs and goals. And, while this magick is also concerned with psychological transformation and spiritual growth, even the spiritual life must be built on firm material foundations.

Here are techniques that will help you to a better life, will help you attain things you want, will help you in your personal growth and development. *Moreover, these books can change your life, dynamically, positively!*

We've always known of seemingly super-normal achievements, often by quite ordinary people. We are told that we normally use only 10 per cent of our human potential. We are taught that faith can move mountains, that love heals all hurt, that miracles do occur. We believe these things to be true, but most people lack practical knowledge of them.

"Psychic powers" and magickal practices can, and should, be used in one's daily life. Each of us has many wonderful talents and powers—surely we have an evolutionary obligation to make full use of our human potentials! Mind and body work together, and magick is simply the extension of this interaction into dimensions beyond the limits normally conceived.

All things you will ever want or be must have their start in your mind. In these books you are given practical guidance to develop your inner powers and apply them to your everyday needs. These abilities will eventually belong to everybody through natural evolution, but you can learn and develop them now!

The Llewellyn Practical Guide to

ASTRAL PROJECTION

The Out-of-Body Experience

Denning & Phillips

1996
Llewellyn Publications
St. Paul, Minnesota 55164-0383, U.S.A.

SECOND EDITION
Twenty-second Printing, 1996

Cover art by Tom Canny

Library of Congress Cataloging-in-Publication Data
Denning, Melita.
    The Lllewellyn practical guide to astral projection /
by Melita Denning and Osborne Phillips.
    ISBN 0-87542-181-4
    1. Astral projection. I. Phillips, Osborne, joint author.
II. Title. III. Title: Astral projection.
BF1389.A7D46   133.9′2   79-88141

Llewellyn Publications
A Division of Llewellyn Worldwide, Ltd.
P.O. 64383, St. Paul, MN 55164-0383

For Sandra Weschcke,

who has smiled at the sun's rising and setting

CONTENTS

Study Points

1

In Astral Projection, the conscious mind is aware of what goes on, but from a perspective that is different from that of the physical body, which remains passive.

Astral Projection—the Out-of-the-Body Experience —is natural, and happens spontaneously more often than you realize. The goal of this book is to show you how to do it AT WILL, and under CONTROL, in order to benefit from the special powers of the astral body.

Astral Projection enables you to function in two different ways:

I. In relation to the Material World:
   a. To travel to any place, and experience material world events;
   b. To undertake special "at-a-distance" works—such as absent healing;
   c. To meet and communicate with other out-of-body people.
II. In relation to the Astral World:
   a. To see and investigate the underlying "behind-the scenes" level of things;
   b. To effect change, first at the astral level, and then—as a result—at the material level: Magick.

Astral Projection and the Art of Living.

Our thoughts and feelings already bring about changes at the material level by their effects in the astral, most commonly in a negative and haphazard manner; but we can work in a positive manner and counteract negative tendencies of this kind, by functioning OUT-OF-BODY. By making astral projection a common experience, you will live life more fully and effectively: with this increased awareness, you make constant use of two principles:

   1. Mind can influence the body to greater health.

2. Mind can control the body in special and unaccustomed ways.

Astral Projection brings about greater integration of the whole person as you experience:

I.   The Will working through the rational mind.
II. The Rational Mind working through the astral body.
III. The Astral Body working through the physical body:
     Neither Will nor Mind work directly upon the physical body—but only by means of an astral or an emotional link.
     Changes at the astral level can be affected by the interaction of the astral body with both the Rational Mind and the Physical Body.

Corresponding to certain points on the physical body are the "Centres of Activity," or Chakras, which form GATES between the levels of existence. These Centres are energy globes connected to the astral counterpart of the spine.

THE ART OF LIVING

1

This book is about *Astral Projection,* which is often —with more exactness—called *Out-of-the-body experience.* By each of those terms, we mean the condition in which the physical body is passive, as if sleeping, while the conscious mind is aware of what goes on but from a different viewpoint from that of the physical body.

This book is also to tell you *how to achieve that kind of experience AT WILL.*

You may quite likely have met someone who remembers having such an experience, at least once or maybe more often. You may have had such an experience yourself, without quite knowing how it came about. Many people are almost sure they have had an experience of this kind, but cannot be totally sure because in their recollection it is mixed up with dream material. To many other people, however, a definite out-of-the-body experience has occurred quite spontaneously and naturally—

BECAUSE OUT-OF-THE-BODY EXPERIENCE IS QUITE A NATURAL THING TO HAPPEN.

Being able to leave your physical body at will— and there are in the world many people who can do this—has great advantages and opens up all kinds of interesting and exciting possibilities for you. In general terms, these possibilities of astral travel are of two kinds.

First, there is the kind which, in the nature of things, you more often discover or hear about: that is the kind of experience in which people move about on earth, seeing friends, carrying out various works such as healing. You can, in fact, look into any matters which concern you. You can enjoy the sunrise from stupendous mountain summits, you can walk through the jungle without fear of being bitten by poisonous snakes or of falling into a swamp; or (because you are not limited to the dimensions of your physical body) you can look into and partici-pate in all the marvels of the living world of nature, if they deeply interest you. You can meet other people who are out of their bodies and hold conversations with them, you can go anywhere you desire and you will discover you can do this without having any idea of the route!

Then, there is the other kind of adventure, in which you travel, not in the material world but in the astral world which is just beyond the material world. We shall have more to say about this soon; but it means that you are "behind the scenes" of the material world, and can see and examine much more deeply into the underlying state of things. Sometimes, if you wish, you will be able to change things at that level—*and the result, as you will afterwards see in your everyday life, will be A REAL CHANGE ON THE MATERIAL LEVEL.*

Repeat: *the result will be A REAL CHANGE ON THE MATERIAL LEVEL.*

Do you realize what this can mean for you?

There are two more facts which we should like to state, now, about that aspect of astral projection. One of these facts you will understand better after considering the nature of the different "worlds," which we shall describe in the course of this first chapter. It is, that *the "higher" the level from which you can bring about this change, the better and more lasting are its effects in the material world likely to be.*

The second fact is, that it is quite natural for people to work in this way upon the causes of events that take place in the material world. It is so natural, indeed, that *we do it to some extent all the time, without even leaving our bodies.* Unfortunately, when acting in this way, we generally do it weakly and clumsily without much idea of what we are about; and, as can frequently be seen, there is a danger that by thinking too much in the wrong way, we may bring about the very thing we are anxious to avoid.

Fortunately, it is in our power to counteract any tendency of this kind—

BY GETTING OUT OF OUR BODIES AND WORKING *STRONGLY* ON THE PROBLEM, AT A LEVEL WHERE WE CAN SEE WHAT WE ARE DOING.

But looking behind the scenes at the causes of things can have a much greater value than simply enabling you to alter them. In fact, as you gain more experience, one definite result will be that you will learn to live in your daily life in such a way that there will be less and less that needs changing at other levels. *You will be learning the Art of Living*—and of living YOUR particular life so as to be YOU TO THE UTTERMOST.

All this, besides having the real fun and delight of

mastering the art of Astral Projection.

You have all the necessary equipment.

In psychological writings, the human psyche—that is, the non-physical part of a living human being—is usually described as having "conscious," and "unconscious" or "subconscious" areas (according to the writers' background of training). From our point of view, it is a good idea to state at the outset that the term "unconscious" only means "not within the awareness of the central consciousness," and to recognize that a life-function thus called "unconscious" may "know" very well what it is about at its own level. Such, for instance, is the process by which we go on breathing whether we are awake or sleeping, or the process by which the "unconscious" parts of the psyche can keep sending highly symbolic messages in dreams to the "conscious" sleeping mind, until it both remembers and understands.

In the ordinary present-day human adult, consciousness during the waking state is more or less limited to the following:

(1) Dim awareness of mental images and abstract notions in continual flux.

(2) Deliberate structures of thought, partly rational, partly emotive.

(3) Intermittent awareness of sense data, passed by the nerves to the brain and thence arising to consciousness.

(4) Intermittent awareness of instinctual reactions, these coming to consciousness as physical sensation and/or emotion chiefly when the instinct is both aroused and frustrated (as in feeling hungry or angry).

This continuum of experience based on mingled inner and outer conditions, builds up a conviction that the consciousness is "contained within" the physical body, and sometimes even a belief that the consciousness is one with that body. We see through the bodily eyes, and if we close our eyes we cease to see; we hear through the bodily ears, and ear-plugs if we use them will deaden the sound; a pain in hand or foot seems to come from the direction we know the hand or foot to be in, although on waking from sleep we can be mistaken about this. If we want to see what is behind us, we turn our head; if we want to see something in the next room, we go bodily and look.

But supposing you are not an ordinary present-day adult. Supposing you are a baby who wants to know if his mother is in the next room? Supposing you are a primitive man who wants to know what goes on outside the cave at night?

You want to go and look. But to take your physical body would be in the one case impossible, in the other case highly undesirable. Yet, if you want strongly enough to go and look, in either case you can.

Young children easily take their consciousness outside their physical bodies. Primitive people do it.

Solitary prisoners sometimes do it too. *You* can do it;
you have only forgotten how. Modern means of
transport and communication have helped you to
forget, and, worst of all, somewhere along the line
you have probably been told that it's "impossible."

Nobody has told that to the primitive man, so he
goes ahead. Nobody has told that to the baby—yet.
The prisoner has left off caring what anyone told
him, he just naturally uses the faculties which
couldn't be taken away from him.

Pure consciousness has two ways of being aware
of something outside itself. One of these two ways
can be put right out of the picture at once, because it
is the "direct intuition" which only belongs to the
highly developed mystic (quite a different thing
from the "intuition" which people may have about a
friend's illness or an impending disaster, but that
doesn't come into our present inquiry either). The
normal human way for consciousness to work—and
"out-of-the-body" experience is *totally* normal and
human—is for it to work *through* a "vehicle" of some
kind.

We already know how consciousness works
through the five senses (sight, hearing, smell, touch,
taste): how it works *through* the nervous system and
brain of the physical body. So how else is it able to
work? To answer this, we need to know what else
there is in all that makes up a person, that the
consciousness can use as a vehicle.

Here, it will be interesting and useful to introduce

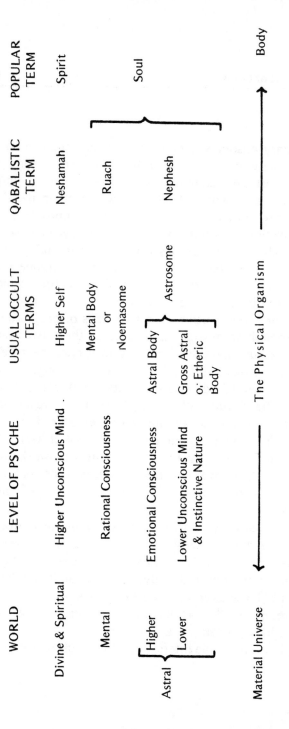

WORLD	LEVEL OF PSYCHE	USUAL OCCULT TERMS	QABALISTIC TERM	POPULAR TERM
Divine & Spiritual	Higher Unconscious Mind	Higher Self	Neshamah	Spirit
Mental	Rational Consciousness	Mental Body or Noemasome	Ruach	Soul
Astral — Higher	Emotional Consciousness	Astral Body	Nephesh	
Astral — Lower	Lower Unconscious Mind & Instinctive Nature	Gross Astral o: Etheric Body		
Material Universe		The Physical Organism		Body

a few words from the mystical and occult tradition of the Qabalah; this venerable wisdom has been found to correspond with the researches of modern psychology, showing an accurate agreement of findings combined with a fruitful contrast of approach and purpose. The diagram on the facing page gives all the terms we shall be using in these pages in connection with the psyche. It shows, for instance, how the popular term "soul" covers several quite different levels and functions of the psyche; an advantage of the more "occult" terms is that they help us to be more precise in saying what we mean.

Like all diagrams, this could mislead on one point while it makes other points clear. The mistake would be, to infer from this classification of the physical and non-physical components of a human being, that the parts which are here identified carry out their special functions quite independently of one another. This is in no case true. *The union of all these components in the one human being* is the most important fact indicated in this chart, and, indeed, the more free and open the flow of energies between the various levels, the better a person is equipped for astral projection as well as for other mind-body adventures. We know that there can be "negative" interactions: unrelieved tension from emotional causes can produce stomach ulcers, while, in the other direction, eating something that upsets the liver can temporarily block the creative imagination. But these hazards can be avoided, and their possibility is more than compensated by the glorious rewards we can gain from the interaction of the levels within our being. A conscious intimacy with the Higher Self is not required for these purposes, but a happy confidence that *it is there,* and a healthy acknowledgment of the reality of high spiritual values, will always help in maintaining our balance in life. It can be a reminder which will enable us to cut earthly cares down to size, and sometimes, it can also convey a hint to the rational mind that the rule of intellectualism is not entitled to be absolute. Below the level of the Higher Self, however, the relationship between the rational mind, the emotional and instinctual mind, and the physical body, needs to be cultivated so that communication between them remains as open as possible. We shall return to this subject with some practical action for you in Chapter 3.

This inter-communication between the various levels of life within you has always been recognised by occultists as having great importance, and nowadays it is also the subject of much valuable medical research. It is being established scientifically how the mind can bring the body back to health and can keep it healthy; and also how the instinctual levels can be trained by the rational mind so as to control the physical body in special and unaccustomed ways, such as are needed by astronauts in space travel, for example.

Having emphasized the necessity of interaction between the various parts indicated on our diagram, and value of encouraging and increasing that interaction, let us consider these parts separately.

The usual outer vehicle of human consciousness is the physical body. It is part of the material world: it has weight, volume, dimensions. It is composed of the elements of the material world; it breathes the atmosphere of the material world; it is nourished upon material food.

If we want to create outward expressions of our ideas, our physical hands, muscles, eyes, ears, assist us to interpret the mind's plan in material terms. The mind is "the artist," but the body handles tools and materials to produce a painting, a sculpture, a book or something else which is also part of the material world. Even a musical composition—the most "ethereal" of artistic creations—is made up of a sequence of atmospheric vibrations produced by instruments of wood and metal, in accordance with a complex series of lines and dots upon paper. Or if we had never learned to read or write, but made songs and sang them extempore like the minstrels of old, our songs would still be made up of vibrations of the air, caused by the vocal organs of the physical body.

In other words, if you want to create something in the material world, you use the fabric of the material world itself, and you work by means of your material body and senses.

Now we come to consider the next level of existence, beyond the boundary of the material world. Here we have a more "inner" vehicle of consciousness, the *Nephesh*, to give it its Qabalistic name. This is the whole of that area of the psyche which makes itself known through the instincts and emotions, forming a broad link between the physical body and the rational mind. As a vehicle of consciousness it is often called the *Astral Body* or *Astrosome*; and just as the physical body is part of, and functions in, the material world, so the astral body is part of, and functions in, the astral world.

It is not easy to give a short description of the astral world. Just as the material world contains a wide range of phenomena, from matter as dense as or even denser than lead or granite to the delicate atmospheric wave-vibrations of sound and color, so the astral world has near-physical forces such as poltergeists which can lift and hurl rocks, and also has high manifestations of beauty and tenderness which most people would term "spiritual." In fact, the contrasts are so great that the astral world is frequently thought of as being divided into two: the higher astral and the lower astral. However, as all the worlds to some extent flow into one another, it seems unnecessary for our purpose to analyze them as subdivisions. The astral world is a region of great power and fascination, with much that is inspiring and exciting as well as beautiful and astonishing. The experienced astral traveller can do important things there as an alternative to simply moving about in the material world. (See Chapter 7, *Adventures in the Astral Worlds.*)

Our own astral bodies, which are part of that world, show a similar wide contrast in their different parts. Here too, we can, if we wish, distinguish between the lower level, the gross astral or etheric, which meshes with the physical body, and the high emotional levels which are closely linked with the mental level of the psyche. Nevertheless, all these functions belong to the astral body, they can and should be directed (not persecuted) by the rational mind, and they are all part of YOUR PERSONAL ASTRAL POTENTIAL.

The mental level of the psyche is termed the *Mental Body*, or *Noemasome*; frequently called the *Mental Sheath* because it is so much finer—more delicate and more penetrating—than the astrosome. The noemasome comprises all that which in the Qabalistic system is understood by the *Ruach*: the rational mind, and the governing consciousness (which is aware not only of the rational mind but also, to a variable extent, of the subrational factors of emotion, instinct and bodily sensation), and the decision-making function of the rational mind.

You may already, at some time, have tested the interaction of these different levels. You may have been occupied in a quite ordinary pursuit, in a familiar situation, when suddenly some message is conveyed to your brain which has connotations of fear for you: maybe the sound of gunfire or a smell of burning. Or you may have been performing an unfamiliar or difficult task, when an unforeseen complication arises: like crossing a chasm by an unsafe bridge, when suddenly another traveller steps onto the bridge at the far end. What do you do? Probably in any of these cases, you send a swift message to your instinctual self: *"Steady, now!"* And why do you do this? You do it so that your physical body should not be moved to any clumsy or unconsidered action by that lower part of your astral body which is engaged with the nerves, glands and blood of the physical body; and so that the directing power remains with the rational mind, *which formulates the dictates of the will.* This is a direct and spontaneous example of re-affirming and strengthening the interaction between the levels, and, too, of establishing the natural order in those levels: the will working through the rational mind, which controls the astral body which acts through the physical body.

Why wait for an alarming crisis to become aware of this interaction? It is going on all the time during your waking life. You will be given (in Chapter 3) a more magical practice for increasing the flow of energy through your whole personality, but you can benefit more easily and quickly from the magical practice if you also give attention to the every-day activities which (although to a lesser degree) bring about the same kind of thing. *It is a definite law of life, resulting from this close interaction between the levels, that a physical or astral manifestation in the personality to which attention is given, will increase in quality or quantity.* There are a few exceptions, as with any law (trying to train the sense of smell is one) but for the great majority of phenomena it holds good, and it is the basic reason why we are told "practice makes perfect."

But now let us look at another example from daily life. Supposing you sustain some small but inconvenient injury, such as a sprained ankle or a cut finger. It causes no continuous pain, you can forget it most of the time, but now and then when you try to make some accustomed movement it stops you, with a sudden sharp reminder of its presence. What is your immediate reaction?

Maybe you impulsively direct annoyance, frustration, anger to the already damaged area—"that darn finger!"—much as if it were an inanimate obstacle in your way; you may not be doing much harm in this, but it is a waste of opportunity. The finger or ankle, as a physical structure, didn't anyway want to be injured. Some unconscious part of your astral level let this happen, from whatever motivation; this in itself is a sufficient signal to the rational mind to take charge particularly of that situation. So how about sending, through the astral level (which means doing it by such things as visualization, emotion, the imagination of a current of warmth and so on) a good wish, a blessing, an image of healing to the site of an injury?

If you do this, you will not only be doing some real good to your body (and the more practice you have, the better it will work); you will also be:

a) giving your will some practice in working through your rational mind,
b) giving your rational mind some practice in working through your astral body, and
c) giving your astral body some practice in working POSITIVELY upon your physical body.

This is good for all levels, collectively and separately.

An important fact which shows up in this, is that *each level of the personality has to work through the one immediately above or below it.*

That means it is no use, for instance, using "willpower" alone to bring about a change at the material level, not even in one's own material level, one's own physical body. People who sincerely claim that they can do so, and who truly seem to do so, generally have a very strong (even if unconscious) *emotional—* that is, astral—drive in support of the supremacy of their will. But, one way or another, if the will or the intellect is to cause any change in the condition of the physical body without using physical means, then *there has to be an astral link.*

Similarly, if we want to cause a change in the astral body, this has to be done by means of the rational mind, but it will be generally more effective if the physical body is involved in the procedure, *so as to work up to the astral level as well as down to it.*

(And can the physical and astral levels in any way influence the mental level? Strangely, but certainly, they can. We see intelligent people all over the world, producing logical arguments to support the most diverse opinions in religion, politics, morality. If any of them change their attitude, it will not be because their reasoning is proved faulty, it will be because of a change in their emotional approach to the subject.)

Coming back to the subject of the astral body, we may consider how far it can be imagined as an exact replica of the physical body. In a sense it is an exact replica and there is certainly no harm in imagining it as such (although as a general principle we should do well to picture it always as a particularly strong, youthful and healthy replica) but a vital feature of the astral body must here be pointed out.

There are certain points in the physical body which have an evident and special affinity with more than the material level. A powerful emotional shock can act like a physical blow upon the solar plexus; either the blow or the emotional shock could cause loss of consciousness. The same is true of the top of the head: "they sat as if stunned," is said of people who have received startling news, and sometimes pleasant news can stun as much as unpleasant, if it is startling enough. Different emotions can render a person for the time being literally "speechless," or "choked with emotion"; while the various emotional states associated with the heart are by no means only metaphorical. We know what is meant when someone is said to be "warm-hearted," "great-hearted," "good-hearted," nor is this idea limited only to one language. To say that a person has been "encouraged" is to use a word that comes to us from the French, and it means exactly the same as to say he has been "given new heart." (French *coeur* = "heart").

Another important meeting-place of the astral and physical levels involves the sex organs; the power of either physical or emotional stimulus here to produce effects both physical and emotional, is too well known to need further elaboration.

There is a also a further important centre, in the middle of the forehead between the eyes, at the site of what is sometimes called "the Third Eye"; this is involved in the higher mystical development of the psyche, referred to in the ancient Chinese system of Tao as "the opening of the Golden Flower," and, even without such a complete development as that, it is employed spontaneously by many people in "seeing with the mind's eye." In the physical body, this corresponds to the position of the pineal gland.

At each of these points that we have mentioned there is, in the physical body, a particular nerve centre or glandular centre. All of them, therefore, even at the physical level are concerned in essential life functions; and because they involve the psyche as well, at its instinctual, emotional or mystical levels, we should expect them to have important counterparts in the astral body.

These counterparts exist, and indeed they are most important. They are not, however, mere replicas of the physical organs.

Corresponding to the physical points which have here been mentioned (and to other points in the physical body as well), there are in the astral body certain distinctive "organs," generally called Chakras or Lotuses in Oriental occult systems, and "Centres of Activity" in Western systems. Like their physical counterparts, these Centres of Activity are vital GATES between the levels of existence.

Besides the everyday practice we have recommended, of keeping the "lines of communication" open by "talking" in friendly fashion to your astral body—and even to your physical body—there is a much more powerful and "specialized" practice which we shall give you in Chapter 3, for the purpose of strengthening these Centres of Activity and increasing the flow of energy between them. The reason why this practice is not given at once, now, is because you will derive more benefit from everything that you do in your training, if you understand better *why you are doing it*. If you read these early chapters carefully, you will understand very well the reason for each step you take and, therefore, you will be able to take it more effectively.

You can, for the present, think of these Centres of Activity simply as globes of ENERGY manifesting as white light, and about two inches in diameter. There are others besides the ones we have mentioned. For instance, that at the base of the spine, employed in the East, does not come into our work, but there is one at the instep of each foot which is important in our system of working, although for convenience we generally picture the two foot centres as one and call it the "earth centre." There is also a corresponding centre in each hand, important in some types of magical work but not for purposes directly necessary to Astral Projection.

These globes of energy do not just "float" freely in the astral body. They are connected with the astral counterpart of the spine; and the astral counterpart of the spine is certainly the most important energy channel that we have.

At this stage, a rather peculiar question may occur to you: from time to time one hears of apparitions which have every sign of being authentic, not always by any means apparitions or "ghosts" of people who have left this world, but quite often apparitions of people still living in their earthly bodies. You hear of people seeing an apparition of maybe a close relative or a friend who was for some reason deeply concerned about them at the time, who wanted to give some warning or some piece of news, or simply to be assured that all was well with them.

Such a figure can be seen in dreams, or—usually only for a fleeting instant—while the person who sees it is awake. Such a figure may be only faintly seen, or for so short an interval that no details could be recalled, only the plain recognition. Or it may be seen quite clearly and distinctly. But never has anyone recorded the sight of such a figure showing anything like Chakras (the word means "wheels") or Lotuses or globes of energy anywhere on the face, head or body. When spiritually evolved people are seen (and sometimes even when they are seen in their ordinary physical presence, in certain circumstances) there may appear a light around the head or around the whole figure, or light may seem to proceed from hands or feet (sometimes being interpreted by the rational mind as "jewels") but, in no case is an astral figure seen with actual "Chakras" or "Centres of Activity."

If these are genuine apparitions (and in some cases we must say they are), and if the Astral Body really has these Centres or Chakras, (and it really has) then why do these Centres not show up clearly in these apparitions? We need not suppose they would look exactly like the "spheres of energy" that we visualize, but we would expect them to be definitely there.

Surely these apparitions are astral?
Yes, they certainly are.

Surely they are sent out by the persons whom they resemble (and who, maybe, afterwards admit to having felt the appropriate emotions, even if they did not clearly know that they were DOING anything)?

Yes, these apparitions are sent out, consciously or otherwise, by those persons.

Then they are the astral bodies of those persons?
No, they are not exactly that.

The next chapter will explain more about the astral vehicle.

Check Point

1

• *Get into the habit of directing messages of love, goodwill and encouragement to your instinctual and physical self, especially when suffering pain, sickness, stress or fatigue. Make sure all such messages that you send are* strong, reasonable *and* positive.

The Art of Living

Personal Notes

The Art of Living

Study Points

2

In its usual state, your consciousness has three vehicles:

1. The Physical Body;
2. The Astral, or emotional, Body;
3. The Mental Body.

In Astral Projection, part of the astral body (the "gross astral") remains with the physical body to keep it functioning, and part of the substance of the astral body goes forth, with or without the conscious mind.

This astral substance can be ejected from the astral body in four different ways:

1. Involuntarily, and without consciousness;
2. Involuntarily, and with consciousness;
3. Voluntarily, and without consciousness;
4. Voluntarily, and with consciousness.

It is the fourth type that is taught in this book, although the other types are described; and special uses for the third type will be given.

Answers to common questions:

1. What happens if you get lost?
2. Is time the same?
3. What about dangers to health?
4. Can you be attacked in the astral?
5. What if the body is disturbed during projection?
6. What are the limitations to projection?

YOU AND ASTRAL PROJECTION

2

We have already seen that the normal human way for consciousness to be aware of anything outside itself, is through a vehicle of some kind.

We have seen that in its usual state the consciousness has three vehicles:

- The physical body,
- The astrosome, or astral body,
- The noemasome, or mental body.

We have also seen that in the normal life of human beings (and in this book we are ONLY concerned with what is normal, we are NOT concerned with anything which is "supranormal" or suited only to demigods or highly developed mystics) the means by which the conscious mind is aware of what is outside itself, is its astral vehicle and usually at the same time (at least, in waking life) by means of its physical vehicle.

The astrosome, however, is less limited. The astrosome has its only awareness at its own level, whether the rational mind knows about it or not. Indeed, the rational mind can be, and frequently is, only made aware later of something which has already been privately transacted by the astrosome, with or without collusion by the physical body. That accounts for a good many situations when the astrosome insists on expressing an emotion which the rational mind would not permit, and the results can be very laughable or embarrassing, according to circumstances.

With regard to the sleeping state, this independent action of the astral level is characterized by the subsequent recollection of a dream which contains a certain amount of vivid and objective subject-matter, but no evidence of more than emotional guidance—and probably also, a mixture of quasi-physical with apparently fantastic or symbolic imagery. This dream evidence indicates that the astrosome can not only act independently of the noemasome but also can have out-of-the-body experiences independently of it. That brings us back to the question we left at the end of the last chapter: *What is it that projects?*

What goes out from the physical body is not—not as long as earthly life lasts—the whole astrosome, the whole astral body. If the whole astral body is ejected, that is death: as in some cases of sudden and extreme shock (as from bomb blast) in which the bodies have shown no sign whatever of a physical cause of death. But such an accident could not occur to a healthy person from any cause less than that type of shock. The entire astral body does not, in out-of-the-body experience, detach itself from the physical body: *the gross astral, at least, remains to keep the heart beating, the nervous system and brain ticking over.* Those essential functions may sometimes be "slowed down" to an extent sufficient to frighten an uninformed observer who sees the unconscious body, but they are continuously and adequately functioning.

A woman traveler, motoring alone through a country district in Scotland, had a mishap to her car which could not be put right until the next day. As it was late evening, she went to an isolated cottage nearby and asked if she could spend the night there.

The cottage was occupied only by an elderly woman and her unmarried daughter; these two told the traveler she was very welcome to stay, save that they had but one bed, which they shared, and they could only invite her to sleep in it with them. Having little choice, she accepted.

During the night she awoke and found to her horror that the elder woman lying next to her was cold, limp, and so far as she could tell was no longer breathing. Hastily, she roused the daughter, with a distressed, "I think something's happened to your mother." The younger woman leaned over, assured

herself of the true state of things, and casually replied
in her broad Scots accent, "Nae, nae! She'll be oot
an' aboot!"

And in the morning before the weary guest was
again awake, the old lady was back from her wander-
ings and was cooking the breakfast.

What goes forth from the physical body in projection—deliberately or otherwise, alone or with the
conscious mind—is *some* of the substance of the astral
body. More, or less, but some; and only some while
life lasts.

ASTRAL SUBSTANCE, then, can be ejected from
a person's astrosome in four possible ways.

(a) *Involuntarily, and WITHOUT the rational
consciousness.* This can have various consequences:
the material may return, or may partially return,
bringing vivid but bewildering and inconsequent
dreams and frequently a feeling of being "more tired
on awaking than on going to bed." (A rather coherent
example is given in the Appendix of this book.) Or
the material can produce strange "poltergeist-type"
rappings in the bedroom; or it can simply be lost and
cause a mysterious exhaustion. Causes and cure of
"astral bleeding" will be completely explained in
Chapter 3.

(b) *Involuntarily, and WITH the rational con-*

sciousness. A book of case-histories could easily be filled with examples of this. Some individuals have almost a habit of "waking" into full consciousness, but into an already unconsciously exteriorized astral vehicle instead of into that which remains in the physical body. Most of the examples one hears of, however, are of experiences during sickness (such as a fever), after a sudden impact (such as a fall from a horse), or while undergoing total anesthesia. The person reports having felt complete, rational and normal, and generally has only been made aware of the situation by recognizing his or her physical body. An example is given in the Appendix.

(c) *Voluntarily, and WITHOUT the rational consciousness.* This is a special magical technique in which material is sent out deliberately, for the purpose of assimilating impressions. Full details of two distinct forms and uses of this procedure will be given in Chapters 4 and 5.

(d) *Voluntarily, and WITH the rational consciousness.* This is the main activity which this book is to teach you.

The chief aim of this book is to explain to you, and to give you all the facts you need on how—

—TO HAVE YOUR RATIONAL CONSCIOUSNESS
FUNCTION *THROUGH—*
—AND TRAVEL AT WILL *IN—*
—A VEHICLE OF ASTRAL SUBSTANCE—
—EXTERIORIZED BY YOU FOR THAT
PURPOSE!

Everything else in this book is for the purpose of
letting you know more clearly WHAT you will be
doing, or WHY various procedures are helpful, *or
HOW you can obtain maximum benefit from your
new knowledge.*

The explanation continues.

The rational consciousness, when this is in the
body in the ordinary everyday state, acts through the
astrosome to draw upon sensory brain-consciousness,
and so builds up its awareness of the physical world.
The brain is not the intelligence, but it is a very complex computer, and the rational mind is to a great
extent dependent upon it for reliable working data; at
least, in some fields of activity. That is why a person
who has not long been practicing astral projection may
have the impression that less than his whole rational
mind is functioning while out of the body. He will be
capable of experiencing his travels distinctly and
definitely, appreciating adventure and excitement and
beauty; forming impressions and judgments of any

human or non-human entities that he may encounter: he may realize that some of his experiences have spiritual significance, which he will interpret, naturally, in accordance with the extent and the type of his own inner development. Yet, with all this, he may not be able, until he gets back to his body, to remember some technical data he thinks might be useful, or to co-ordinate his astral experience with an earthly experience of the same sort that he knows he once had.

This however does not indicate any limitation in the mind's own capability while in a state of projection. It is simply a temporary effect of its separation from the brain's computer-bank. Many people who begin astral projection may *never* be troubled with this problem; but those who are, will find that the trouble passes away altogether when the projected state becomes, with practice, part of the normal life-experience.

Can you recall how, when you were a small child, you needed years of practice to learn to use that physical body, and then to learn to use that brain? If you don't remember any of it very clearly, you may have watched other people going through it all in their childhood: tumbling about while learning to walk, then struggling to hold a pencil, then really working hard to do simple arithmetic *and to memorize how to do it?*

Anything you need to learn now will be a great deal easier than that, and for two reasons.

Reason One: You have heard of the "Inertia of Matter"? Well, your astral body is far quicker and more tractable than your physical brain!

Reason Two: You will find that owing to the particular nature of astral travel and astral adventure, a lot of the brain-clogging stuff that seems necessary in physical life would be just plain useless in the astral! (One example of this was mentioned in the previous chapter—you will not need road-maps).

Of the kind of knowledge that you do need to carry over into your astral experiences, or that you wish to carry over because it means a lot to you without perhaps being strictly necessary, you will find that as you become more and more accustomed to projection, more and more of that material will, in fact, be carried to the deeper levels of the psyche so as to be available to you in the projection state. That will happen altogether painlessly and with nothing of the struggles of the small child at school, *but it is useful to remember that child* so as not to be too impatient with yourself or to expect to be able to do everything at once without any practice.

But the practice itself is fun. Like learning a new sport: the joy of a sudden improvement, a new success on the way. Like a sport, too, astral projection is achieved by developing faculties WHICH ARE YOURS ALREADY.

It may be, however, that having read this far you still have some questions, of the sort that people very often ask us. Before starting in on the actual training that will lead you into achieving out-of-the-body experience, it is a good thing to make sure there are no lingering worries in the back of your mind about it. Besides, *when you can do astral projection*, you may wish to tell someone about it (it isn't desirable to talk about it beforehand, unless to someone who can already do it or to someone who will be learning at the same time as yourself). And the other person is quite likely to ask some of these questions; so even though you yourself may have your mind very happily made up about the whole matter, it is advisable for you to know the answers and to think about them yourself so that you can see how they work. When you have your own astral experience you can reinforce the answers from that, but these answers will give you a beginning.

Question 1. Supposing when you are out of your body you get lost, or forget how to come back?

There is no possibility of either of these things causing any problem, because you are not dependent on the rational consciousness to look after them for you. When you are an experienced astral traveler you will know how to "will" yourself effectively to go to any place that you have particular reason to go to, and your own body is the place that you supremely have particular reason to go to. And *until* you are an experienced traveler, you will find that your one besetting problem is not "how to get back," but "how to stay out"; you will find yourself liable to click back into your physical body for the least reason, often when there is no external reason at all but only a transient idea.

In addition to this tendency—and in fact, it is a reason for this tendency—the astral vehicle that you will have made for yourself will not be entirely free from the astrosome which remains in your physical body. There is always a tenuous connecting "cord" of very fine astral substance. Sometimes this is referred to in occult books as "the silver cord." That phrase is taken from the Old Testament, the Book of Ecclesiastes Chapter 12, Verse 6, where "the silver cord is broken" is given as a metaphor for death: the astrosome having gone forth completely and finally from the physical body, there is no longer that connecting link. That concept should not, however, cause us to think of the connecting cord as anything weighty or bulky, even in astral terms. Many people have performed astral travel very effectively for years without ever being aware that they were in any way connected to their physical body meanwhile. If you know the "cord" is there, and you look for it when you are out of the body, you will probably be able to see it, and this may be reassuring to you. But even if you don't see it, you can be certain it is functioning just as effectively.

Two things more about the "cord." It is not just a safety device. With practice, you will find ways of pulling "more strength" or "more knowledge"—as you may need—to your conscious self when out of the body, *through the cord.*

And because it is only a delicate strand of your own astral substance, it is simply re-absorbed on your return.

Question 2. Supposing when you are out of the body you lose track of time, and don't attempt to come back for months or years?

We know there have been rare cases—*nothing to do with willed and conscious astral projection*—in which a person has gone from normal sleep into a cataleptic state, lasting very occasionally for years. Never have these people been practising any form of occult training: we can say that confidently because the doctors, searching earnestly for some demonstrable cause of this strange occurrence, would certainly have made much of the fact of occult training, had there been any.

In the methods we are giving you in this book, there is plenty of material to ensure a healthy and plentiful flow of energy between the various levels of your psyche *and your physical body,* even before you begin direct work on astral projection. For a person in a reasonable state of health there is no danger of an abnormally long or damaging state of catalepsy resulting from any of the recommended practices.

As to "forgetting the time," of course to some extent that happens. Here again there is a self-operating safety device. In the astral states nearest to earthly consciousness (that is, the states to which the inexperienced will be limited until they are ready for further progress) there is a definite sense of time: in fact, this is one of the ways in which you can distinguish between an astral experience and a mere dream, for in a dream it is hardly ever a definite and true time of day or night. As you become more experienced, you will be able to go to more "timeless" regions, but by then you will be more perfectly in command of the situation anyway.

In any case, remember—the gross astral, that part of your astrosome which is in closest contact with your physical body, *is still there when your consciousness is elsewhere*—and it is at the bodily end of the connecting "cord." *When your body wants you back, your gross astral will pull you back, never fear!*

Question 3. You have mentioned that there is no danger in astral projection for a person in "a reasonable state of health." Are there states of health in which you would DEFINITELY NOT recommend a person to attempt astral projection (out-of-the-body experience)?

Yes, there are. These practices should not be attempted by sufferers from: *Heart disease of any kind; High blood-pressure; Any serious affliction of the nervous, circulatory or respiratory systems.*

Minor ailments seem, however, very often to be rather ameliorated, not only by projection but also by the preparatory practices which are given in this book, simply because these practices tend to raise the general bodily "tone."

Question 4. Supposing you—your conscious mind in your astral vehicle—are attacked by something evil while away from your physical body?

The term "something evil" can be accepted in this context without question. We generally feel that anything which causes us suffering, distress or inconvenience is "evil," especially if we see no sort of reason for the assault (whatever kind of assault). In any case—in the comparatively uncommon case of being attacked in one's astral vehicle by an astral entity—no-one splits hairs over it. One is attacked: one defends oneself.

How serious are these astral combats? They do seem to be totally serious when they happen, and there is adequate evidence that these incidents are true astral occurrences and not nightmares. But as an incarnate human being you have an enormous advantage, in that *all the levels of existence are open to you, from the terrestrial to the divine.* You can, literally, escape to another world from your attacker. You can drop back into the physical, as Robert A. Monroe describes himself as having done, in the chapter "Intelligent Animals" in his book *Journeys Out of the Body* (page 143), or you can force the fight up to a higher astral level as the anonymous woman narrator evidently did in one of the Histories in *The Triumph of Light,* Book IV of THE MAGICAL PHILOSOPHY (page 241). On the whole, the technique of going higher is more to be recommended, as such vicious entities are, by nature, of the lower levels; they can thus be thrown off and discouraged from further attack.

So you see, if you have aspirations as a modern knight errant (or lady errant) there is still the chance of an occasional brush with a "dragon" on the astral. But no-one kills anyone and it IS adventure.

Question 5. Supposing your physical body is disturbed or molested while your conscious mind is away from it?

The dangers of this situation have been greatly over-stated by a few writers. Remember: the gross astral does not leave your physical body while your consciousness goes traveling; and the gross astral is the deeply instinctual part of your psyche. It is a good watchdog. If a burglar comes to your house, the gross astral will pull you back to your body just as quickly as it could arouse you from ordinary sleep at such a time. On the other hand, if someone who is well disposed to you tries mistakenly to wake you— be it mother, spouse or friendly landlady—there may be no success whatever, and your body may even be taken by the shoulders and shaken—such things have occurred!—without bringing you to wakefulness in the material world. The gross astral knows that no harm is meant. As for the dangers from shock in such circumstances, so long as the traveler is not suffering from any of the physical conditions given in the answer to Question 3, these dangers appear to be imaginary; or, truly, they are no greater than the dangers of awaking from ordinary sleep to confront the same disturber.

What does matter in learning astral projection, is to make as certain as possible that you will NOT be disturbed. Nothing is more difficult than to form your astral vehicle and exteriorize your consciousness into it, *if you are expecting at every moment that someone may walk into the room!*

Question 6. If you can go where you like in out-of-the-body experience, how about looking around military sites?—or going and reading some top-secret documents? If people can do what you claim, none of those things can be really secure.

In one sense, no "secret" on earth can be *really* secure! Military sites and secret documents are usually safe against any normal material hazards; and upon examination, the astral hazards turn out to be less than you might suppose.

You can go wherever you *desire* in your astral vehicle; this is not the same thing as being able to go where you *like*. The vehicle in which you travel is ASTRAL, and therefore is governed by emotional, not intellectual considerations. Even if you make your astral vehicle go to a place in which you have only an intellectual interest, your mind is still dependent upon it for awareness of what is outside itself: *The mind has to work through a vehicle of some kind*, and so is dependent upon the co-operation of that vehicle.

When in the physical body, you can make yourself read any uninteresting stuff, because the computer of your brain (which was programmed in your childhood) will "scan" it for you, whatever the subject-matter; even at that, your astral (emotional) level may be so unhelpful as to prevent you from remembering what you have read. When you are out of the physical body, you don't even have the computer action of the brain to help you. Reading anything at all is difficult to most astral travelers: reading something which has no personal interest is virtually impossible. The same with the topographical details of places visited.

Of course, there are people of a different sort, the

"astral drifters" who may find themselves almost anywhere without any volition whatever, but they need cause no apprehension as they neither know nor really care what they may chance to see—"My dear, I dreamed I was in such a funny sci-fi sort of place!"

Still, there is another and more serious side to the question. Just because a subject is without emotional appeal to many people, you cannot assume it is without emotional appeal to the whole human race.

Probably most politicians, if during a bodily sickness they found themselves free to travel at will in the astral, would fly straight away to the kind of place they would wish to spend a vacation in: blue skies, delightful surroundings and their favorite hobby. But a famous and incontestable case of astral projection concerns a British Member of Parliament, Dr. Mark MacDonell, who was not only seen and recognised in the House of Commons on two days while his body lay helpless in bed, but also, when during that time a vote was taken on a measure which deeply interested him, *he recorded his vote in the approved manner.*

As to reading secret documents, there have been admitted instances of students travelling astrally and seeing authentic questions in the exam paper they were to answer the next day. Not the whole paper; not, usually, whole questions, but vitally important parts of questions. Vitally important *to those students*; hardly interesting reading to the population at large.

So the astral traveler can, if he has a sufficient desire to do so, pass through locked doors. Maybe those exam papers were guarded only by locked doors and, once the doors were passed, were clearly visible?

Here is another example, from the realm of "dreaming true"—a kindred subject to out-of-the-body experience or astral travel, since nobody can draw a clear line between them. When any person dreams true about a matter which cannot be arrived at by telepathy between person and person, where is the source of his knowledge?—he must surely be able to look into some level of things beyond the material level? The astral, then?

This story concerns one of the pioneers of paleontology in the nineteenth century, a man who was entirely occupied in researching the early history of this planet by means of the study of fossils and rocks, at a time when scientists not only knew far less than they do now, they also had far less technical equipment with which to work. One day he was working on a piece of rock from which, at one side, layers had been removed to reveal the head of a fossil fish. Our scientist was much interested in this, because the head showed it was a different kind of fish from anything previously discovered. He wanted to chip away enough of the rock to reveal the whole of this fish. But how could he do this without fear of damaging part of the all-important relic, when he had no idea of its size or shape?

No matter how he though about it, he came back
into the same circle of ideas: he would have to chip
away the rock to see what the fish looked like, in
order to be able to chip away the rock without
damaging the fish.

There seemed to be no solution to this, so he
went to bed at last and fell asleep wondering about it.
And he dreamed he did indeed chip away the rock,
and he saw what the fish looked like.

When he awoke in the morning, he remembered
the details of this dream, which had been singularly
vivid. So he resolved to act upon it, and to assume the
mysterious fish looked as he had seen it in his dream.
This enabled him to chip away the rock confidently
and successfully: and the fish looked just as he had
seen it in his dream.

However this example works—and there could be
several possibilities, but there is no purpose in
theorizing about them here—it is certainly clear that
our scientist gained access to the knowledge he
wanted *through levels of consciousness other than the
material,*

and

*he gained it because it was a matter of intense desire
to him.* The work he was engaged in was not just a
"job"; to him, it was his life.

In experiences of that type—"dreaming true" or
unmistakable astral projection—people gain only that
knowledge which is "theirs to know," which is part
of their life-pattern.

If anyone has that sort of passionate and intimate desire to know an official secret, it is on evidence a definite possibility that he may achieve the astral reading of it.

But people who take up out-of-the-body experience for the joy of it, will probably decide upon things they would a hundred times rather do, on each and every occasion that they "go out"!

Check Point

2

- *Remember to direct messages of love, goodwill and encouragement to your instinctual and physical self. As you become accustomed to doing so, you will find any number of little occasions during the day when you can send such a message by a quick act of the will, rather than waiting until your lower self is actually signaling distress!*
- *Can you think of any questions about Astral Projection besides the ones that are answered in Chapter 2? If so,* write them down. *Then read through Chapters 1 and 2 again, to see if this helps you think out the answers for yourself. If it does not, keep your questions by you, and consider them again in the light of each chapter* after you have read it.

You and Astral Projection

Personal Notes

You and Astral Projection

Study Points

3

Preparation for Projection:
1. Live as naturally as you can!
    a. Dietary considerations——there is value in a limited/vegetarian diet.
    b. What's good for the physical body is good for psychic and spiritual well-being.
    c. The need for exercise.
2. Practices:
    a. Time and Place: select a place where you can be free of disturbance, and use it on a regular schedule for all your astral projection work.
    b. Use of a "rite for setting-apart" as an aid and a protection.
    c. The locations of the Centres of Activity in

relation to the body.
d. The Postures:
   • Wand, or standing.
   • Earth, or lying.
   • Egyptian, or sitting.
e. The Rhythmic Breath.
3. *Formula One—to energize the Six Centres of Activity.*
   a. Wand posture.
   b. Rhythmic breath.
   c. Sequential visualization of the Centres (and their colors).
   d. Drawing down the Light.
   e. Circulation of the Light.
4. The Solar Plexus, the Seventh Centre, as the GATE from which to eject astral substance for various purposes.

ASTRAL PROJECTION IS NATURAL

3

Now you are going to make a practical beginning on your real work for astral projection.

How long will it take you to achieve success in it? —weeks, months or years? Or will you take to it "like a duck to water" as soon as you know all about it?

You can help yourself to achieving out-of-the-body experience sooner rather than later. *And everything you do will help you to live a healthier, happier, better life altogether.*

Remember: OUT-OF-THE-BODY EXPERIENCE ——ASTRAL PROJECTION——IS NATURAL!

Therefore, while you are learning to achieve it, *live as naturally as you can.*

And—not only to keep up your ability to project at will, but for your great benefit in every way besides—go on living as naturally as you can for the rest of your life!

What does this mean to you *now*?

First there is the question of DIET.

An examination of all the outstanding evidence regarding astral projection, shows the desirability of *an abstemious diet*.

This does not mean you should starve yourself. It means, don't overeat. Find out what you need, *in terms of real food*, and keep to it. Most people nowadays in the Western World eat too much—and why? With few exceptions, we all need to expend less energy in daily living than did our forebears, so why the need to eat extra? The trouble comes from the fact that most people eat "junk foods" with little or no goodness in them, so of course the body demands a greater quantity.

Eat only good food, and you will need less. *Aim* to eat less: there are plenty of publications to guide you in choosing sensible foods. You DON'T need "sugar for energy"—it is a useless burden to the system—and you DON'T need "all the protein you can get." We couldn't live without protein, certainly, but neither do we need all the protein that is available to us. Growing children need it, to build larger bodies; but do *you* want a larger body?

This may puzzle you a little, because in the first chapter of this book you have read of the benefit of having free-flowing energy passing easily among the different levels of your psyche and body: it may seem to you that eating more food would give you more of that energy. It wouldn't. *Energy locked up in layers of fat is not at all free-flowing, it takes a lot of painful effort to release it.*

If you are, or can be, a vegetarian, that is all to the good! It is all part of living as a natural human being. Frankly, Man is in some way a "hybrid" creature, with the teeth of an *omnivore* (eater of flesh and of vegetable substances alike) and the intestines of a *herbivore* (vegetarian). This means that our teeth and our intestines alike are designed to cope with vegetable foods, *but only our teeth are designed to cope with meat!* So from the point of view of physical well-being it seems obviously best to be a friend to one's intestines and to be totally (or mainly, according to one's practical possibility of choice) a vegetarian.

And as you are not a body plus a psyche acting in dissociation from one another, but a composite human individual, doing your best in this way for your physical well-being *must also be doing your best for your psychic and spiritual well-being. Theories apart, the facts also demonstrate this.* Inevitably, people can quote a few instances of great mystics or thaumaturgists who have been meat-eaters or who seem from their legends to have been meat-eaters. But taking the testimony of the whole world, East and West, from the time of Pythagoras onwards, the vast majority of visionaries and wonder-workers—those who have gone up to the heights, and those who have brought spiritual force to bear on earth-level—have been vegetarians.

Next to the subject of diet comes that of EXERCISE. This is particularly important because, from ancient times, it has been a well-observed fact that if "psychic" and earnest-minded people have a typical fault, that fault is sheer physical inertia—they tend to keep their activity to the non-material level.

Unfortunately, this concentration if carried too far can defeat its own purpose.

Circulate That Energy!

Walk, swim, jog, climb, do isometric exercises or the old-fashioned "daily dozen"—what you please—but do *something* that necessitates your not only giving your body a regular ration of active movement, but also giving it your attention and encouragement. This is a vital part of the "interaction of the levels" of which you have read already in this book.

SOON, IN THIS PRESENT CHAPTER, YOU
WILL BE GIVEN AN IMPORTANT MEANS OF
CIRCULATING ENERGY FROM THE HIGHEST
LEVEL OF THE PSYCHE. THIS IS A MOST
POWERFUL PRACTICE, *but you can make it even
more powerful FOR YOURSELF if you put in your
own practice of circulating the energy of the physical
body, at some other time in the 24 hours.*

So now you are ready to begin considering the
main sequence of practices which are to lead into
astral projection itself: these practices in which,
certainly, your physical body will participate, but in
which the principal action will take place in your
mind and in your astral body. You should provide
carefully for these practices.

Where are you going to do them?
And when?

(THEY SHOULD BE DONE AT THE SAME
TIME AND PLACE THAT YOU INTEND FOR
YOUR FIRST EXPERIENCES IN PROJECTION
ITSELF, if that is humanly possible).

For a lot of people, there can only be one realistic answer to those questions: "In my bedroom, at night." That's fine.

For a lot of other people, early afternoon might be the one time they can be sure of a couple of hours alone. That's fine, too.

Or perhaps you have a special meditation room, dressing room, boudoir or gymnasium of your own, into which it's taken for granted you can disappear at any time you may arrange? That's ideal!

No matter where it is, however, three things should be definite:

(1) While you are learning, you should always do whatever practices you intend in the same place.
(2) You should always if possible do them at the same time every day (or night).
(3) And—even if it means waiting until the rest of the household is asleep—you should be certain of not being disturbed.

Wherever the place is that you intend for this activity, *and whether or not it has to be used at other times for other purposes*, it will be a good thing if you devise and perform a little rite of "setting apart" that area, *as far as this special activity is concerned.* Maybe some of the "set apart" or "blessed" feeling may spill over into the other activities that the place is used for, but that can't do any harm, can it? The important thing is that that special influence will be there to give the place a distinctive peacefulness and security when you use it for the purpose for which you have marked it by your little rite. Never mind how brief the rite may be. It will work, if—

- You keep it simple.
- You only use signs or words that you really believe in.

What sort of thing can you do?

You can imagine that a kind of luminous white-ness comes out of the end of the longest finger on your right hand (left hand if you are left-handed). That isn't "make believe," because you *can* give out astral energy in that way, and for this sort of purpose, when you want to. And with it, you can "mark round" the boundary of your chosen area. Join it up neatly.

Having done this (and "seeing" the line if you can, or at any rate mentally knowing it's there) say— out loud if possible—something like: "Here shall enter

only the Powers of Light, for to the Light I aspire."
And towards each of the sides of the area, trace in the
air a cross or a star, or *whatever sign means protection
to you*. If you don't feel you have such a sign, trace a
second protective boundary in the air, above the first
one and *going round in the other direction*. Join that
one up neatly too.

In any normal circumstances, doing this kind of
rite once, before ever you begin to use the area for
your projection practices, should be sufficient.

NOW TO BEGIN THE ADVENTURE OF REAL ACTIVITY WITHIN THIS AREA.

In the first chapter of this book, you have a short
account of the Chakras, or Centres of Activity—with
particular notes on the six major Centres which are
used in modern Western work on personal development. You may like to look again at that passage
before going on with this new material.

Here is a list of the bodily positions corresponding
to these six Centres of Activity, but in a different
order from the way they are given in the first chapter:
here they are in order from the top down:

Crown
Brow
Throat
Heart
Sex
Earth.

It has been mentioned already that these Centres are imagined as spheres of energy, each about two inches in diameter. Now they can be given more precision. *For the present, each Centre of Activity should be visualized as a globe of white light, about two inches across,* in the following positions on the central vertical plane of the body:

Crown	A little distance above the top of the head, not resting upon the head.
Brow	At the mid forehead and as if half inside the head, half outside.
Throat	Completely outside, just in front of the thyroid cartilage.
Heart	At mid chest, and as if half inside, half outside.
Sex	At the genital region and as if half inside the body, half outside.
Earth	The feet being placed with their inner edges just or nearly touching, this Centre is visualized as being half below the ground-surface and half above,

slightly interpenetrating the feet at about the region of the insteps.

DO NOT ATTEMPT TO VISUALIZE ALL THESE SIMULTANEOUSLY BEFORE BEGINNING THE PRACTICE.

THE POSTURES

Three Postures are used for the various techniques and practices in this book. In each case, you will be told which to adopt:

The Wand Posture: This is an upright but not stiff standing posture; the head is held erect and looks straight forward, the shoulders are "dropped back" to give a balanced and comfortable stance, the arms hang relaxed at the sides. The feet are parallel, their inner edges touching or almost touching.

The Earth Posture: The "supine" position, flat on the back. If the spine is very much arched in the lumbar region, the knees may be slightly bent to counter this; the head also is tilted slightly towards the chest so as to give the back of the head more stability. The arms are extended at the sides, the legs are placed together.

In complete relaxation, the feet will naturally fall outwards, but in normal waking consciousness a slight degree of tension is generally maintained to avoid the possible discomfort of this.

The Egyptian Posture: As in the ancient statues, this seated posture has the spine vertically balanced, the palms of the hands resting upon the knees or thighs as may be more comfortable, the thighs horizontal and touching, the lower legs vertical and the feet side by side planted evenly upon the ground. *The chief secret of performing this posture successfully, is to provide yourself with a comfortable chair or stool of exactly the right height; if this cannot be had, a seat-cushion or a footstool should be used to make good the discrepancy.*

See photographs on pages 82, 83, 84.

IMPORTANT NOTE: NEVER, IN ANY PRACTICE CONNECTED WITH PROJECTION, SHOULD ANY POSTURE BE ADOPTED WHICH INVOLVES CROSSED LEGS OR ARMS. THIS RULE CAN HAVE NO EXCEPTIONS.

The above postures are so simple they hardly require practice, but they should be noted for reference.

THE RHYTHMIC BREATH

Here, by contrast, is something you can hardly practice too much. Do it anywhere and any time, by day or by night. Begin it, then tell yourself to continue it while giving your attention to some other pursuit; note if you are still doing the rhythmic breath a half-hour later, for example. Go to sleep doing it. *For general practice of this* you don't need to keep strictly to the three postures just given, but have your spine as straight as you can, and DON'T CROSS YOUR ARMS OR LEGS.

The Rhythmic Breath has many uses besides the ones in this book. It can aid long periods of mental concentration, because ordinarily without it you find you have from time to time to break off a train of thought so as to start up your breathing again. It can aid in all kinds of sports. It has both bodily and psychic value. It can steady nerves, boost energy, and, as you will learn here, it can help you *direct* energy. That, again, opens up many other purposes it is good for.

PRACTICE

RHYTHMIC BREATHING

UNTIL IT BECOMES A HABIT

AND MAKE IT AN ALLY FOR LIFE.

The way to do it: First put any noisy timepieces right out of your hearing. Then take up the Egyptian posture. (For your first-time-ever experience of rhythmic breathing, it is advisable to be strict about this. Apart from other reasons, it feels so good that you'll want to try to get as nearly as possible into that ideal posture whenever you practice rhythmic breathing in a sitting position, whether at your office desk or reading the morning paper, or anywhere else. And that's good for you.)

Next, identify and give attention to your heartbeat. This can be surprisingly elusive—you have probably been deliberately ignoring it for a number of years—so if you have difficulty with it, find a pulse in your throat, temples or wrist. As soon as you can keep track of the rhythm, begin counting beats. Now you can experiment, to find your own Rhythmic Breath.

What you are aiming to establish, is a pattern of breathing in which you can comfortably hold your lungs full of air for a certain number of heartbeats, then breathe out during *twice* that number of heartbeats so that your lungs are as empty as you can comfortably make them, keep your lungs empty for the *original* number of beats, then breathe in during the count of the double number, your lungs being well expanded at the end. And so on. To make this clear, here are three examples, one of which is almost certain to be yours:

Hold lungs full during	Breathe out during	Hold lungs empty during	Breathe in during
2 beats	4 beats	2 beats	4 beats
3 beats	6 beats	3 beats	6 beats
4 beats	8 beats	4 beats	8 beats

In connection with astral projection, it makes no difference whatever which of these breathing patterns you make your own. Don't strain after the higher figures! At the same time, it is true that with practice you may find that the pattern just naturally changes; for instance you may begin with 2-4-2 and find after a while that your breathing capacity has increased so that now you are more comfortable with 3-6-3. That is fine, but for practice purposes you must *keep the rhythm of the breath*: until you can comfortably hold your breath both "in" and "out" for three heartbeats, you should NOT extend your inhaling or exhaling time over six heartbeats. Wait for another week, and most probably you will find that you can do the 3-6-3 rhythm correctly and comfortably.

The reason for this care is that this good and safe breathing rhythm that you are learning *is not the only breathing rhythm that has significance.* To upset the rhythm is like tapping at random on a Morse key: your signal might mean *anything!* So keep your experiments within the range of the rhythm given. But if your natural breathing capacity gives you a pattern of 1-2-1 or of 5-10-5, you're unusual but O.K.

Now we can begin putting these various practices and techniques together.

In a scientific work of any kind—in chemistry, in physics or mathematics—when a number of substances, or ideas, or processes are put into the correct sequence to produce a particular result, the statement (in words or symbols) which shows that sequence is called a *Formula*. What you are about to read now is a *Formula*. It is very simple compared with formulae given for the same purpose in other books, but there is good reason for this. This book is PRACTICAL, and the only thought-material in it is as much as you need to conduct YOUR PRACTICAL ADVENTURE IN ASTRAL PROJECTION successfully.

This Formula therefore has been stripped of everything which served only to label it as belonging to this or that School of Thought, AND RETAINS ONLY ITS GREAT POWER.

FORMULA ONE

To energize the six Centres of Activity.

(To be performed in your chosen Projection Area.)

Stand upright in the Wand Posture, establish the Rhythmic Breath. *(Stand there, just doing rhythmic breathing until you feel quite settled into it.)*

On an "out" breath, become aware of the Crown Centre as a sphere of intense whiteness. *(Don't rush this; if at first the presence of the sphere of light above your head is not "real" and shining to you, go on as if intensifying its brightness with several further breaths. And so with the other Centres when we come to them. Be aware of them as clearly as you can: they are sure to become brighter and more clearly defined with future occasions.)*

On an "in" breath, draw down a shaft of white light from the Crown Centre to the middle of the forehead.

On an "out" breath, become aware of the Brow Centre. *(Formulate it as clearly as you can—placed just as described on page 67 —and also continue to be aware of the Crown Centre and the connecting shaft of light! Again--and so with all the Centres— give this formulation TIME.)*

On an "in" breath, draw down a shaft of white light from the Brow Centre to the middle of the throat.

On an "out" breath, become aware of the Throat Centre. *(Take especial note of page 67 for the placing of this Centre; and again keep a consciousness of the Crown Centre, the Brow Centre and the connecting shaft of light.)*

On an "in" breath, draw down a shaft of white light from the Throat Centre to the middle of the chest.

On an "out" breath, become aware of the Heart Centre. *(Keeping consciousness now of the Crown Centre, the Brow Centre, the Throat Centre, and the connecting shaft of light.)*

On an "in" breath, draw a shaft of white light down from the Heart Centre to the region of the genitals.

On an "out" breath, become aware of the Sex Centre. *(Keeping consciousness also of the Crown Centre, the Brow Centre, the Throat Centre, the Heart Centre, and the connecting shaft of light.)*

On an "in" breath, draw down a shaft of white

light from the Sex Centre to the ground between the insteps.

On an "out" breath, become aware of the Earth Centre. *(You should now be aware of all six Centres, all spheres of white light positioned as described on page 67, and connected by a shaft of brilliance. Draw three or four rhythmic breaths as you contemplate these Centres, part of your inner being, brought into greater awareness and radiance by the light you have brought down from the Crown Centre, which in itself is a symbol and manifestation of your Higher Self . . .*

. . . then let that image fade as you turn your consciousness to a new visualization. From the Earth Centre bring upwards again a jet of white light which ascends to just above your head, divides, and descends just outside your arms. Passing beneath your feet, the two columns join, to ascend again as before. There is thus a continuous fountain of dividing, reuniting and circuiting light. Maintain this last image only for a few complete rhythmic breaths, then let it slowly fade. After five rhythmic breaths, all images should be gone.)

You should practice this Formula daily for two

weeks at least, exactly as given above; and for a
longer time if that is needed for the action to run
smoothly without reference to the text, and for the
Centres to be visualized as bright and well-defined.
The final "Circulation of Light" is an essential part
of the Formula, and is to be included every time
the Formula is performed.

When you are satisfied with your performance
of it, a further development can be brought into your
use of the Formula. You can visualize the Centres of
Activity in color. When this is done, although you
may have reached a state of proficiency so that
you can complete the white-light formulation
without delay, still you should always devote several
rhythmic breaths to each sphere for the colored-light
formulation.

The colors for the Centres of Activity are as
follows:

Crown Centre: White brilliance, like burning
magnesium.
Brow Centre: Glimmering soft dove-grey.
Throat Centre: Billowing intense mid-purple.
Heart Centre: Pulsating radiant yellow.
Sex Centre: Pure lavender, radiant and fast-
swirling.
Earth Centre: The seven prismatic colors,
swirling lazily and shimmering.

The connecting shaft of light is always white and brilliant; remember the power it brings down is from your white brilliant Crown Centre, which links you to your Higher Self.

Whether practicing with white light or color, always visualize the Centres as spheres of about two inches in diameter, and in the positions given in the list on page 67.

The practice of Formula One, in either white light or colored light, will confer upon you many benefits; when you are so familiar with it that you feel you need not do it daily, AT LEAST continue it three times a week. If you have become so attached to it that you want to go on with the daily practice of it, that is excellent both for your general well-being and for the progress of your work towards astral projection.

YOU WILL GAIN from the regular use of this Formula:

(1) A strengthening of the Centres of Activity themselves, and of communication between them. This means that when you actually begin projection, you will have—

> (a) A ready flow of psychic energy available AT WILL when you desire to form your astral vehicle.
> (b) A ready interaction between the levels, both

for such actions as "pulling along the cord" reserves of power or of knowledge when you are out of your body, and for assimilating the experience of your astral travels when you have returned to your body. That last is important, because without such ready inter- action, even though you may remember your astral adventures perfectly, *the physical brain may still struggle to reject them* as "unreal" and may impose some degree of "shock" upon your nervous system—all because your body didn't have its accustomed place in your experiences!

(2) A means of circulating energy in your psycho- physical system, so that any which cannot be utilized at one level can be re-distributed to the others. This is a very good method of safeguarding against the disorder known as "astral bleeding" which is mentioned in Chapter 2; but if there is reason to suppose that a person may already be afflicted with astral bleeding, the practice of Formula One in a regimen which also includes some form of daily physical exercise and a frugal diet—the very conditions you should adopt for your astral projection training— is highly recommended.

The reason for this lies in the cause of astral bleeding, namely *a surplus of energy, at astral level, that is not under the control of the individual person- ality.* To prevent or to correct this, it is important to avoid any accumulation of energy at one level, or of astral or physical substance, and to circulate energy through all levels under the direction of the will. At the same time, the recommended regimen will preserve the total energy of the individual from wastage, and over a period of years the good results of this *are very perceptible* in health, in mental vitality and in general youthfulness.

It is impossible within the scope of this book to go into all the reasons for these great benefits, but the way to secure them has been known to the wise men of East and West for many centuries, and can be equated with LIVING THE NATURAL HUMAN LIFE AT ALL LEVELS.

YOU AREN'T GOING TO MISS ANY HAPPINESS THAT WAY!
YOU ARE GOING TO HAVE THE MOST FUN, AND THE BEST ADVENTURE, THAT THERE IS— —THE JOY OF BEING YOUR REAL SELF, IN ALL THE WORLDS!

AND IT IS ALL PART OF YOUR PROGRAM FOR ASTRAL PROJECTION.

THE SOLAR PLEXUS CENTRE

If you have looked into Oriental systems of personal development—and many of us these days have done so to a greater or lesser extent—you may have wondered in your reading of the foregoing chapter, *Why only six Centres of Activity?—why leave the Solar Plexus Centre out of the list?*

First, as we have pointed out, the number seven is, although traditional in the East, not representative of the number of Centres or Chakras existing. We could not use all there are. The six Centres which are listed in this chapter are those whose direct activation is essential for modern Western development. If this is done, those not listed will be indirectly activated and general equilibrium will be maintained.

The region of the Solar Plexus, that is, the upper abdomen, is, in the system we are setting forth, the region from which astral substance is ejected for various purposes: including that of making your "vehicle" for projection. Because it has this special use and activity, to activate it by means of Formula One also could cause imbalance among the Centres.

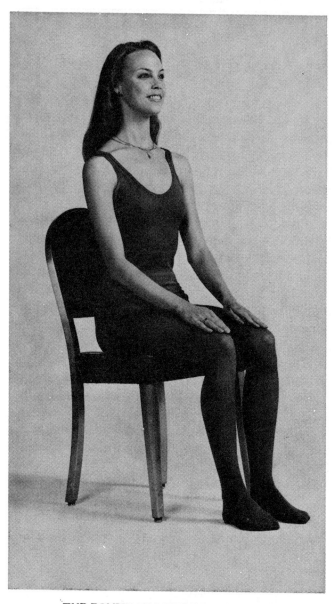

THE EGYPTIAN POSTURE — See page 69

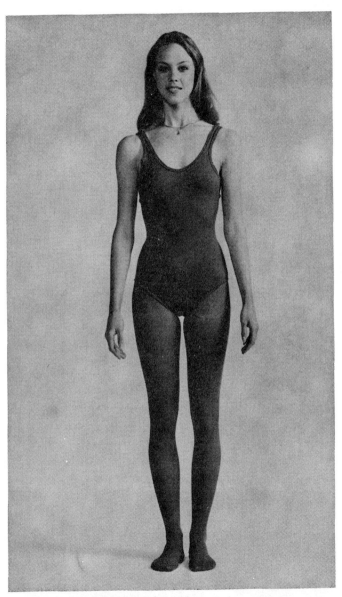

THE WAND POSTURE — See page 68

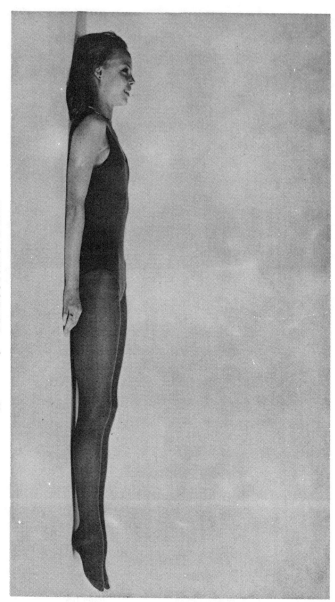

THE EARTH POSTURE — See page 68

Check Point

3

- *There is a lot of practical work in this chapter. Make a start on it promptly but take care to plan with care where necessary. THIS IS YOUR NEW LIFE.*

- *You will probably want to revise your diet to some extent; there are good books that you can read about it. Whatever changes you make,* keep them within your capacity. *You can always progress further at a later stage!*

- *The same with exercise. After physical exercise you should feel your powers have been tested, not exhausted. Have sufficient sleep but don't overdo this either. AND—REMEMBER?—BE A FRIEND TO YOUR LOWER SELF!*

Now we come to practical work that is specifically part of your Astral Projection program:

• *YOUR PROJECTION AREA. Choose it and "set it apart."*

• *THE CENTRES OF ACTIVITY. Learn these so that you locate them in relation to your physical body without the book. Take special care with Crown and Throat Centres!*

• *THE POSTURES:* Wand Posture, Earth Posture, Egyptian Posture. *Make sure you can do these exactly: we give photographs to help you.*

• *RHYTHMIC BREATHING. Practice as described in the text.*

• *FORMULA ONE. This is the foundation of all your astral practice.* You will gain by every care you can give it.

• ABOVE ALL, TAKE ALL PRACTICES CARE-FULLY AND IN ORDER!

Astral Projection is Natural

Personal Notes

Astral Projection is Natural

Study Points

4

Projection of Astral Substance:
1. Greet your Lower Self with a smile!
2. Become a trustworthy friend to your Lower Self!
3. Technique for ejecting astral substance:
   a. Your usual time and place for astral projection work.
   b. Wear either loose, single piece clothing, or none at all.
   c. Take no food during previous hour.
   d. Assume the Wand Posture.
   e. Establish the Rhythmic Breath.
   f. Perform Formula One—to energize the Centres of Activity.
   g. Continue the Rhythmic Breath.

    h. Visualize astral substance being exteriorized from the solar plexus centre as a diffuse cloud.

    i. Form substance into a sphere.

4. Turn astral substance back into a cloud, then reabsorb it through the solar plexus; perform Formula One.

5. Advanced work with a "key figure."

    a. Technique for ejecting astral substance ("a" through "i" above).

    b. As an alternative to the sphere, form the exteriorized astral substance into a human figure, in the same posture as yourself, facing you, connected solar plexus to solar plexus by a thin silver cord.

    c. Do not, at this time, identify the key figure with yourself!

6. *Formula Two—to send out a "Watcher."*

    a. Technique for ejecting astral substance as in No. 3 above, "a" through "h."

    b. Form the exteriorized substance either into a sphere or the key figure—with preference given to utilizing the sphere, at least in your beginning work.

    c. Turn this shape, i.e. the Watcher, to face the direction in which it will be sent.

    d. Send the Watcher to some place or person of which you wish knowledge; visualizing it going out of your room and disappearing.

    e. Do not repeat Formula One at this stage, but

go about your regular business until the time you have set for recall of the Watcher!

f. At the pre-determined time, enter your working area, assume the posture and re-establish the Rhythmic Breath.

g. Now perform Formula One—to energize the Centres of Activity.

h. Continue the Rhythmic Breath.

i. Mentally summon the Watcher, and visualize it returning to your room; bring it to rest about eight feet in front of you.

j. Dissolve the Watcher into the diffuse silver-grey cloud and then re-assimulate it by 4 above.

k. Assume the Egyptian Posture.

l. Re-establish the Rhythmic Breath.

m. Allow impressions of the Watcher's experiences to rise into consciousness.

n. Record your impressions.

7. Precautions on use of the Watcher Formula:

a. Do not use an animal shape!

b. Always re-assimilate the exteriorized substance!

c. Always pre-determine when the Watcher will be recalled, and do so punctually!

d. Remember that the Watcher's experiences become part of the experience of your astral body.

e. Do not attempt such a practice during the waning of the Moon, or while the Moon has completely waned away.

   f. Also avoid the "dead" period of the year.

8. Perform Formula One every day—morning and evening if you can.

SEEING AND KNOWING

4

$\mathcal{S}$o now let's see where you have arrived.

You should have at least two weeks' practice of Formula One behind you, so that you are reasonably proficient in energizing the six Centres of Activity; although you will naturally go on increasing in proficiency as you go on employing this Formula in connection with further stages of progress in projection.

You should also be accustomed to Rhythmic Breathing, to the extent that it begins to fulfill its purpose, and *instead of keeping your attention fixed upon your physical body, it should help you to forget it when necessary.* You cannot forget your physical body unless the brain and the nervous system are placid, and are receiving a sufficient supply of oxygenated blood for the work in hand.

You should be accustomed to Rhythmic Breathing in all of the three postures—the Wand Posture, the Earth Posture, the Egyptian Posture—because all these will be used, for different purposes, in the different experiments and practices in projection *that you are going to m ;ter.*

Further, you sh uld be feeling particularly fit and positive. Either yo will have adopted, lately, a new abstemious diet and a regular form of physical exercise, or you will ha e a new and exciting reason to maintain the good h its you've already built. Either way, you'll KNOW b now that you are on to something very good, fr n which you can benefit in several very important vays.

Here is a new acti n that you should build into your life-style right n w. You can do this every morning, no matter w re you may be so long as there is some sort of m ror to look in, whether for shaving, brushing your hair, putting on make-up, whatever, in fact, your ki d of body looks in a mirror for. (Some people do th r morning limbering-up in front of a large mirror, an there's a lot to be said for that!) Each morning, whe taking your first look in that mirror, give yourself a real friendly smile and say "Good morning!" Or "Hi!"

Don't look at yourself with a frown that reflects all of yesterday's worries; a lot of mature people do

that, who should know better. Don't peek anxiously
at yourself, wondering if the world can possibly find
you likeable today. A lot of young people do that,
and they certainly ought to know better. *You are
looking at a close and loyal friend*—your physical and
instinctual self—*and that friend deserves and will
appreciate a smile and a cheery word.*

You already send "kind thoughts" now, but a
little later in this book you will learn a way of speaking with your lower self in words, and a way too
of understanding the answers. So begin to form a
closer acquaintance now, when you are riding high on
your new joy-of-life regimen, in the same way that
you would with anyone else whose confidence you
wanted to win: with that good-morning smile and
cordial word of greeting. If you have in the past
discouraged communications from your lower self,
you may have to persevere a little before the response
comes; but otherwise you will begin almost at
once to feel even more happiness and contentment,
because your lower self will quickly identify itself as
the recipient of the message given to your mirror
image, and its return salutation will well up in happy
emotion to your conscious mind. This readiness of
the lower self to identify with the mirror image, with
"that-over-there" rather than "this-in-here," is the
quality which you will be shown before long how to
utilize for your benefit. *Don't*, however, spend time
now trying to analyze or to rationalize it:

Just look in the mirror every morning with that smile and greeting!

This opens A NEW IMPORTANT STAGE in your personal program.

The next new activity for you to begin should be done in your chosen projection area, and at your chosen time when you will not be liable to disturbance. (As you were told in the previous chapter, there is *no need* to repeat at any time the "setting-apart" rite that you performed for this area: but if you would feel happier to repeat it now that you are beginning a more advanced stage of the work, then by all means do it again or re-affirm it. If a repetition would unsettle you, however, don't do it. The important thing is for all levels of yourself, chiefly the deep emotional and instinctual levels, to feel secure.)

You are going to learn to eject astral substance from your astral body: substance which in fact remains *part of you*, but which, while it is exteriorized, can be shaped and directed by you for different purposes. The chief of these purposes, of course, will be to form the "vehicle" for your consciousness when that travels apart from your physical body; but there are other valuable practices which make use of exteriorized astral substance, and you are going to accustom yourself by means of these to directing and

Make friends with your Lower Self.

controlling that substance with full confidence.

You will probably realize, also, that in acquiring these preliminary practices *you are being given the key to much that you may have come across in occult writings* whether these were given as fact or fiction: *much that you may have thought impossible, much that is usually put forth only as "fiction" because so few people would give credence to it.* When you understand the exteriorization and control of astral substance, while that substance still remains part of the person who sent it forth—plus the fact that this substance can be fashioned to any chosen shape!— you will see how simply, how easily, many of the old stories could be true.

To make a beginning, then, you have to be able to eject, or exteriorize, this astral substance. This is not only a matter of *mentally knowing how to do it*; the immediate controller of this astral substance is your lower self, your emotional and instinctual self—the one you give that friendly word and smile to in the mirror every morning—and that guy or gal has to recognize you (conscious, thinking you) as a friend, has to trust you and be willing to work along with you. Further, your lower self has to find the knack (privately, behind closed doors in its own department) of segregating and sending forth the required amount of astral substance *when you want this done.* So there are two sides to this although the team-work is necessarily very united.

Here, then, is the technique:

The place and the time should be those you have chosen for your projection work. You should not be wearing any tightly-fitting article of clothing: nudity, or a single loose garment, are the best options. Neither should you have eaten within the hour: digesting a meal is, in itself, a work for the attention of your instinctual level of being, and if you divide that attention both your projection endeavors and your digestion are likely to suffer.

You stand erect in the Wand Posture, take up the Rhythmic Breath, and when this is established you perform Formula One. (Formula One, as a general rule, is incorporated in all these experiments: in the first part of the experiment, it energizes, and in concluding the experiment it helps prevent astral bleeding and ensures a rightful harmony between the levels.) The Formula having been completed, you continue the Rhythmic Breath.

Now, you are going to bring astral substance out from the "solar plexus" region, the upper part of the abdomen. People do sometimes exteriorize astral substance from other parts of the body or head, but

Ejection of Astral Substance.

the solar plexus is very "astro-sensitive," and it is easiest to work from that area. (To find the exact spot, just ask yourself where in the upper part of your abdomen you feel most *vulnerable*.) So, in your visual imagination, send forth to a convenient distance before you a jet of silver-grey mist, which should form at that distance into a small cloud. Imagine this cloud next forming into a sphere. *Do not visualize any great quantity of silver-grey material being exteriorized*, and when you think—or say— "That's enough!" let the outflow cease; though the sphere should still be attached to the point of ejection by a faint cord of the same substance. (See Chapter 2, *Question 1*.)

For this initial practice, you have now only to put the procedure into reverse. Simply visualize the sphere becoming once more a diffuse cloud, then draw it all back into yourself through the cord rather like drinking through a straw (the Rhythmic Breath will help), then finally re-absorb the cord.

When this process is complete, check that you are still in the Wand Posture and round off your experience with a repetition of Formula One.

The first two or three times that you work through this procedure, you are likely to have an inner feeling that the whole thing is only happening in your imagination. Don't let this trouble you; the first few times, quite likely it *is* only happening in your imagination.

But, quite quickly, your astral body will grasp what you are showing it, what you are expecting it to do, and, unless it has any specific motive to resist your wishes, it will very soon make your visualizations and directions of astral substance *real*. Be ready to sense that first delicate response; take care to be pleased, grateful, to let your lower self know it has done well.

Show, enact, and then when the action is successfully imitated, *manifest pleasure.* An animal, a young child, or the sub-rational levels of your own personality: all can be trained in this way. "Failure" would usually only mean the need for more patience; sometimes, but rarely, the need to discover the reason for a contrary impulse. But in the great majority of cases, patience, kindness, gentleness, confidence-winning are all the qualities required.

You can add something more to this initial practice in ejection of astral substance. Instead of simply forming it into a sphere, try forming it into a "key figure"—that is to say, into a human figure of about your own stature, generally silver-grey in color, clothed in a simple dignified manner, being altogether unelaborate and not over-detailed in aspect. DO NOT ATTEMPT IN ANY WAY TO IDENTIFY YOUR-SELF WITH THIS FIGURE AT THE PRESENT STAGE. It is simply a doll, a puppet, a lay-figure as yet. Visualize it in the same posture as yourself, and facing you. The connecting cord should extend from your solar plexus to the solar plexus region of the figure. When the figure is quite clearly and plainly *there*, then unemotionally turn it back into a nebulous mass of silver-grey vapor, and re-absorb it through the cord in the normal manner. And, of course, don't forget Formula One!

How long should these practice sessions last?

It is impossible to make rules for everyone, but a lot of useful practice can be done in a half-hour if the time is well organized, and no more than this should be taken at present. If the initial visualization is performed without delay, the astral body will become accustomed to doing its genuine work according to the same time schedule; and a regular program also has this advantage, that some sense of time will in fact "get through" to the deeper levels of the mind, thus helping to guard against any over-long tarrying in the Astral World at a later stage.

A most important rule is that no endeavors, whether elementary or advanced, in astral projection should be prolonged after fatigue has set in. It is the physical body, the nervous system, and their integral levels of the psyche that will be fatigued, and *these levels must not be "driven."* To give them a distaste for the practice sessions, or for the authority shown by the conscious mind, harms the endeavor in a way that could not possibly be outbalanced by any seemingly good qualities of determination or perseverance.

When you have reached a degree of proficiency in the practices already given, you are entitled to ask some questions before attempting to launch your consciousness forth in a vehicle of this kind. After all, even if you give it the outlines of a human figure, you cannot endow it with sense-organs, you cannot design for it any adequate equivalent of eyes and ears. How do you know that when you travel in such a vehicle you will indeed be able to perceive or to be aware of anything that may be going on around you? Will you in fact be conscious of the outer world?

There are two ways of answering this. One is the simple theoretical way, which does not really prove anything but which, *after the event,* you will know to be the truth: that is, that all sense organs are merely a kind of "windows" in the earthen body, windows and telephones and the like, which give the psyche the opportunity to acquire data in just those limited ways that the sense organs allow it. The psyche is dependent on them, not by the limitations of its own nature but by force of circumstances.

The other way to answer the question is to give you a technique which will allow you to find out for yourself something of the sensitiveness of astral substance to its material surroundings, *even without the presence in it of your conscious mind.*

YOU WILL REALIZE AT ONCE THAT SUCH A FORMULA HAS A FAR GREATER VALUE THAN MERELY TO PROVE THE SENSITIVITY OF AN ASTRAL SHAPE! HERE FOLLOWS, IN *FORMULA TWO,* A FURTHER MOST IMPOR- TANT PIECE OF OCCULT KNOWLEDGE.

Just as the techniques you learned from the earlier part of this book built towards Formula One, and that formula has helped you towards your new technique for exteriorizing astral substance, so now you will be given an immediately practical use for the practice of exteriorizing astral substance. This, *although it is easier than out-of-the-body experience* to a lot of people, will still be of great use to you even when you have mastered every technique in this book and become a proficient astral traveler. For, although astral travel is an excellent means of finding out what is going on in another place, it is not always convenient to leave your physical body in a state of unconsciousness meanwhile, especially if it is daytime and you have other activities that need your conscious presence.

In such a case, it has long been the custom of experienced occultists, instead of detaching their consciousness from their body, to send a "Watcher" composed simply of their own astral substance to the desired site, to do the surveillance for them while they are conscious in ordinary physical existence and free to pursue other concerns. Two things must of course be remembered:

A *Watcher can only Watch:* that is to say, it can "pick up" anything perceptible to any of the physical senses and any prevailing emotional "tones" at its destination, *but it cannot intervene.*

Also, *a Watcher cannot make any intellectual deductions from what it witnesses;* it is for you to do all the intelligent reasoning and deduction, after its recall.

IT CAN, HOWEVER, GREATLY EXTEND YOUR EARTHLY AWARENESS.

FORMULA TWO

The Watcher

(To be performed in your chosen Projection Area.)

Stand upright in the Wand Posture, establish the Rhythmic Breath.

Perform Formula One.

Eject astral substance from the upper abdominal region, then formulate this into a simple sphere, or into the Key Figure. *(The Watcher can of course be formed into any shape that may be preferred, but there are definite reasons against choosing, as an example, any animal shape, and the beginner will do best with one or the other of the two forms given here. The sphere is recommended.)*

Turning in the correct direction if this is known *(this is not strictly necessary, but helpful)*, by an act of the will SEND the Watcher to some person or place of which you desire knowledge. *(In visual imagination, see it go, out through door, window or wall, disappearing as it goes about its errand. Usually the mental command, "Go to So-and-so," will suffice, but the Watcher's departure should always be witnessed by you. The cord simply fades as it attenuates.)*

(This concludes the first part of the operation. Do *not* repeat Formula One at this stage, but you can very well go now about your ordinary occupations, until the hour at which you have determined to recall the Watcher.)

For the recall, take again the Wand Posture in your chosen projection area, facing in the direction in which the Watcher has disappeared. Re-establish the Rhythmic Breath.

Mentally summon the Watcher. *(Having given the mental summons, make the figure reappear visually, and bring it to rest some eight feet away from you.)*

Turn the Watcher again to a silver-grey cloud, and then re-assimilate it. NOW repeat Formula One.

Be seated in the Egyptian posture for this next part of the action. Re-establish the Rhythmic Breath.

Now, simply allow impressions to rise into your conscious mind as you sit quietly. *(These impressions should be from the returned and re-assimilated Watcher. You will most likely be concerned at first because they come with no label of origin. Are they imaginary, or at any rate are they contaminated with imagination? The only answer, while you are a beginner at this, is to send the Watcher to some person or place which makes it possible for you to check afterwards on the accuracy of your impressions. THE WATCHER SHOULD ALWAYS BE SENT TO GATHER STRICTLY EARTHLY KNOWLEDGE, but even so, erroneous impressions are, from time to time, met with that have a symbolic or other relationship to "other levels." More practice, and the examination by you of as much data as possible, are the remedy.)*

Write out your findings. With practice, it is possible to bring this technique to a point whereby *much knowledge can be gained from it with accuracy.*

Very soon indeed, however, you will have experienced sufficient of its working to be convinced of the complete objectivity of astral perceptions; it is chiefly the interpretation of those perceptions which will need practice. BUT THIS FORMULA ONLY UTILIZES ASTRAL SUBSTANCE WITH ITS INTRINSIC EMOTIONAL AND INSTINCTUAL PERCEPTIONS. WHAT WILL IT BE LIKE WHEN YOUR CONSCIOUS MIND, IN A FULL OUT-OF-THE-BODY EXPERIENCE, IS CONTROLLING A VEHICLE OF THIS SUBSTANCE?

*THE ABOVE FORMULA GIVES YOU SOME-
THING THAT HAS BEEN, THROUGH CENTURIES,
A CLOSELY GUARDED SECRET OF THE
OCCULT ORDERS.*

*THEY DID NOT BELIEVE THAT MEN AND
WOMEN COULD BE TRUSTED WITH SUCH
KNOWLEDGE AS THIS EXCEPT WHEN THEY
HAD BEEN BOUND BY SOLEMN OCCULT OATHS.*

*WE DO NOT THINK THE PETTY SPYING AND
FEUDING AMONG THEMSELVES, IN WHICH
SOME ORDERS HAVE EMPLOYED THEIR
POWERS, HAVE MUCH BENEFITED HUMANITY
OR IMPROVED THE STATE OF THE WORLD.*

*WE PREFER TO TRUST THE INTEGRITY OF
THOSE WHOSE COURAGE, SELF-DISCIPLINE
AND COMMON SENSE ENABLE THEM TO
FOLLOW OUT THE DIRECTIONS CONTAINED
IN THIS BOOK.*

At the same time, there are certain precautions
which you should always observe when using this
Formula, both for your own sake and for that of
other people.

To some of these precautions you may already
have noticed a passing reference.

One is the warning *against forming the Watcher
into any animal shape.* The reason for this is, that
the people most likely to want to employ an animal
shape are those who have some strong affinity,

whether conscious or unconscious, with some specific kind of animal. As such an affinity must also be at the astral level, it could cause some powers associated with that animal to be unintentionally transmitted from the depths of the personality to the Watcher. The Watcher, instead of being a mere passive shape, could then act with some degree of volition and could increase in strength by drawing more astral substance to itself, through the cord. Experience shows that such forms, having acquired some volition and escaped from surveillance, invariably become malicious.

This is frequently true even of astral shapes in human form, if they are not properly controlled by the person who made them, either using them as a vehicle for the consciousness or keeping fairly close contact with them. This is one of the reasons why, when you have made an astral form *in whatever shape,* you must *always take care to reassimilate it* when the purpose for which it is intended has been fulfilled.

Another precaution to be observed in this connection, is this:

Before sending forth a Watcher, *always determine in your own mind the time at which you intend to recall it.* Write this down if need be. Then perform the second part of the formula punctually. This is not only a good discipline as regards the Watcher, it is also a very good means of gradually building up that sense of time in the unconscious levels of the psyche, which will be helpful when you come to the actual projection of consciousness in an astral vehicle.

It is important to remember that when the substance of the Watcher is re-assimilated, its experiences become part of the experience of your astral body; that is to say, ITS experiences become YOUR experiences, at emotional and instinctual level. (This fact will be utilized later in this book, in a different and much more advanced technique, which you will be able to employ for your own further development in many different ways.) Also, *while the Watcher is away upon its mission, it is still part of you, still attached to you by the astral cord no matter how attenuated and imperceptible this may be.*

It is for this reason chiefly that you are advised, at least in the early stages of your work, to form the Watcher as a simple sphere. There is another reason too: you are learning by experience, which is the best of all ways, that astral substance can pick up very accurate information as to what is going on in the material world around it, without the use of eyes, ears and other physical sense organs. But the main reason is that a lot of other people, whether occultly trained or not, have some degree of clairvoyance—some people more, some less. They are in any case less likely to become aware of a plain globe of astral substance remaining motionless in their vicinity, than they would be to perceive the presence of something in human shape. Our whole instinctual nature tends to be alerted by any suspicion that a human shape is present.

If your Watcher is in that way perceived, the purpose for which you sent it may be spoiled—although not necessarily, if you only wanted evidence of the objectivity of the experiment—but there is also a danger that someone with occult knowledge, or acting under the instinctual guidance of sheer panic, might *attack* your Watcher astrally. It could then be sent violently back to you, with the possible consequence of an unpleasant shock to your nervous system. *This is not at all a likely occurrence if you are not seeking to harm or frighten anyone, and if your Watcher is in the simple globe form;* but most people do react strongly against human-shaped "phantoms."

There are two other cautions you should know about, and should heed, although they may seem unduly esoteric. They apply to *any kind of practice with exteriorized astral substance, until you are thoroughly experienced in that particular practice.*

One is: *do not attempt such a practice while the Moon is waning or at the time when the Moon has waned completely away.* You may be aware of the established fact—affirmed anew by the delicate instruments of science as it was by the delicate natural perceptions of our ancestors—of the effect of the phases of the Moon upon the growth of plants. Plants show altogether more growth and vitality through the time of the Waxing Moon and the Full Moon. Now, your astral body has much in common with the vegetative nature of plants: the effects of the Moon's phases are less noticeable in the lives of animals and of human beings simply because these have greater powers of individual volition than we find in plants. But, in anything which is purely instinctual, the Moon rules even human reactions as surely as those of plants.

As a simple example: what is more instinctive than childbirth? Now, any nurse in a maternity ward will tell you, no matter what carefully-calculated dates the various patients may have been given by their doctors, when it comes to the Full Moon, there will be a slight delay on the part of some of the earlier ones, and a slight prematurity on the part of some of the later ones, so that the nurses can always look for a full-moon rush of work with new babies.

A different example can be found in considering the old-fashioned and presently avoided word "lunatic." This word was, strictly, applicable only to a particular sort of afflicted people whose rational mind was not in normal control of their behavior, so that the sub-rational and instinctive impulses were plainly evident. It could thus be seen that their reactions were governed by *Luna*, generally resulting in an outburst of nervous excitement every Full Moon.

We can be sure, therefore, while the Moon is waxing, of a steadily increasing flow of energy and creativity at emotional and instinctual level, that is, at the astral level. During the time of the Waning Moon there is not only a decrease in energy, but also the weakened impulses are more erratic and more difficult to direct: it is like the difference between directing a strong jet or current of water, and trying to control a spreading swamp. That is why, because of these weakened and possibly erratic influences, it is strongly advisable to avoid any work with astral substance during the Waning Moon, until you are completely experienced in the practice in question.

The other caution, for a somewhat different reason, is *to avoid anything involving ejection of astral substance during the "dead" period of the year, that is between December 21st and March 22nd.* This time it is the solar influences which are weak—the Northern Hemisphere is turned furthest away from the Sun at this season—and the influence of the Sun is very much bound up with the rational, controlling mind. The further north you live, the more this matters; while, if you live in the Southern Hemisphere, the position will be exactly reversed, and it is the period from June 21st to September 22nd which is to be avoided.

While we wish the astral energy with which we do these fascinating and exciting things to be strong and vital, we wish our power of controlling it to be strong also, so that we shall truly be directing it and shall not be directed by it.

However, that is sufficient of caution. You have in this chapter learned how to exteriorize astral substance as and when you will, how to control the amount ejected and to form it into a desired shape; you have learned how to send it forth by the Formula of the Watcher, how to recall and reabsorb it, and how to bring to your consciousness the knowledge the Watcher has gathered while absent from you. *Be proficient in these things; this facility in controlling astral substance will open many more doors for you.*

When you are proficient in exteriorizing and in reabsorbing astral substance, you should go on to the Formula of the Watcher at once; thereafter, *and until you begin actually doing the NEXT Formula in this book,* the Formula of the Watcher should be performed *daily,* as far as possible. That will not be totally possible in any case, because of the avoidance of the Waning Moon for example, and there may be some personal reason that prevents you from doing it at some other time. The rule for these times is this:

IF PERSONAL REASONS ALONE LIMIT YOUR PRACTICE, perform *both* Formula One *and* the exteriorization and reabsorption of astral substance, daily if you can but at least three times a week.

IF THE "DEAD TIME" OF MONTH OR YEAR INTERRUPTS YOUR PRACTICES (those times are bad for *all* astral work) then make sure to perform Formula One every day: morning and night if you can. NOTHING should hinder your use of Formula One.

Check Point

4

- *A HAPPY MORNING GREETING to your mirror image each day. (But remember the KIND THOUGHT and WELL-WISHING to your lower self at other times too.)*

- You are regularly using *FORMULA ONE (which includes Wand Posture, Rhythmic Breath, Visualization and Energization of the Centres of Activity, with a subsequent Circulation of Light.)*

- Now you learn *TO EJECT AND TO RE-ABSORB ASTRAL SUBSTANCE, also TO SHAPE ASTRAL SUBSTANCE AT WILL: Sphere, Key Figure.* From this you proceed to:

• *FORMULA TWO: THE FORMULA OF THE WATCHER. This includes sending forth the Watcher, recalling it, and receiving impressions from it. Wand Posture and Egyptian Posture are used.*

Important Reminders:

• *ALWAYS RE-ASSIMILATE ASTRAL SUB-STANCE after the purpose of exteriorizing it has been fulfilled.*

• *WRITE DOWN your impressions from the Watcher immediately:* when accuracy has to be checked it is never good to depend on memory.

• *AVOID astral practices in the Waning Moon and in the dead season of the year.*

• Keep up your HEALTH DIET and PHYSICAL EXERCISE. For all astral practices, wear LOOSE GARMENTS OR NONE.

Seeing and Knowing

Personal Notes

Seeing and Knowing

Study Points

5

Astral Projection is part of your psychic and spiritual growth program:

1. In childhood, much of your natural psychic ability was suppressed, along with many childish fears and feelings. As you now release your psychic self, you likewise release these suppressed fears and feelings, and they may present some problems to you.
   a. Your Lower Self needs understanding and support from the Rational Mind during this time—so continue greeting your Lower Self with a smile!
2. Other problems—really very minor ones—may develop in the same way as the process of

release continues.
   a. Your program of good diet, exercise and continued work with Formula One and the other astral projection practices, provide you with all the ability that is necessary to help yourself.
3. (As your growth continues you will find your new, energized personality may attract people to you who drain away your vitality. Directions are given so that you can avoid this loss, or, equally, so that you can give energy in "healing.")
4. *Formula Three—The Simulacrum:*
   a. Your usual time and place for astral projection work; loose, or no clothing; no food during previous hour.
   b. Assume the Wand Posture and establish the Rhythmic Breath.
   c. Perform Formula One—to energize the Centres of Activity. Continue the Rhythmic Breath.
   d. Reflect upon the relationship between your Rational Mind and your Higher Self—and formulate a deliberate intention that they should be in harmony, working together.
   e. Exteriorize astral substance to a place about ten feet in front of you, and form it into a likeness of yourself, facing you. This *Simulacrum* represents your Lower Self.
   f. Greet the Simulacrum! Address it with

gentle authority, love and concern—as you would a younger brother or sister—on matters of self-improvement. Everything said should express love for the Simulacrum.

g. Thank your Lower Self for helping you in this action, and give it your blessing.

h. Re-assimilate the Simulacrum.

i. Reiterate the resolutions and counsel which you used in "f" above.

j. Perform Formula One.

5. Make a 45-minute cassette tape of these resolutions and play it over each night as you are going to sleep.

6. Keep a Dream Diary—see end of this chapter for a form—and think of your dreams as communications from the Lower Self.

7. Perform Formula Three daily for at least two weeks, skipping Formula Two during this time. Then use either Formula Two or Formula Three at will.

SOUL SCULPTURE

5

$\boxed{\text{E}}$verything should be going well at this stage, but even so, you may very well wish for a general tidying-up of your personal program. Diet, physical exercise and your astral experimentation should all have fallen into a regular place in your daily life. You should at this time be performing Formula Two regularly, and that of course includes a performance of Formula One. But if for any reason you are not using Formula Two for some days, be sure to do Formula One and the exteriorization practice on page 99, at least three times in the week. That is the *minimum* you should be doing at present; but the "Watcher" Formula—Formula Two—ought to be done *daily* at this time if that is at all possible.

However, there can sometimes be some particular

problem which ought to be given attention before we go on.

The range of human possibilities in this area is so great and varied that it is almost impossible to name representative examples. Roughly, they can be grouped in two categories: problems that existed anyway, although they may very well have been brought to the surface by your new program, and problems arising from the program itself.

Either way, it's good to have these things out in the open, and this is a very good time to begin working them out.

Because—remember—this program is NOT ONLY to help you in astral projection. *Astral projection is a natural part of living a healthier, happier, better life altogether.*

That is why there may be a signal, now, from something that doesn't fit in. Sometimes people find in these early stages of projection work that a childhood sense of insecurity or guilt returns, that they thought they had outgrown years back. The trouble is, they hadn't outgrown it, they had only given in to it. People lose their childhood psychism under pressure of attitudes imposed by older people, who in turn were treated in the same way in *their* childhood: usually that sort of thing goes back for centuries. Youngsters give up, suppress and forget the psychic, intuitive, emotional side of themselves—and very

often give up the greater part of their natural
creativity along with it—simply to get from under the
guilt feeling of being "naughty," "silly," "unsociable,"
"introspective" or whatever the particular label may
be. Then when as adults they make an effort to
recapture the suppressed faculties, of course the
emotional and instinctual part of themselves—the
very part they need to work with—is liable to come
up with all the old fears in the original form or a
disguised one—of being guilty, punished, rejected,
unloved, laughed at, in danger of some sort. The
rational mind knows there is no good reason to feel
any of these things, but the lower self needs to know
it too.

And one of the difficulties in that state of things
is that the rational mind probably broke loose from
the other faculties and went on with its own intellectual development independently. The daily "Good
Morning" and smile in the mirror can work wonders,
but some kind of reassurance that is more specific
may be needed.

A quite different kind of difficulty which may be
encountered is connected with the new way of life. It
happens, not uncommonly, that people develop a
recurrent craving for some sort of food they know to
be bad for them; or a person may have given up
smoking, or alcohol, with great success initially, only
to find that a desire for whatever it may be comes

back from time to time. Now, this cannot mean that they have a "real need" of these things. This does not refer to the rehabilitation of alcoholics, which usually requires skilled and specialized medical direction; but it does refer to the many people who could be free of the self-poisoning routines of our civilization, *if they were once convinced that they were doing themselves no favor, giving themselves no "treat," but the reverse, by taking these substances into their bodies.* The purpose here, be it noted, is NOT to turn the happy occasional drinker or smoker off something he or she enjoys, as long as it causes no sense of guilt or of hindrance in living according to one's will. People vary. *Most people will NOT find that a moderate intake of alcohol or of tobacco will prevent their achieving astral projection*; to suggest such a thing in this context would go directly against known facts and instances. *Some people with sensitive systems do, however, find tobacco and alcohol inimical to their progress.* Furthermore, there are large numbers of people who wish to be free of these things, either for the sake of their general health, or for economic reasons, or—very validly—because they resent having had grafted on to their life-style something they feel to be artificial and alien. This is particularly mentioned at this stage because, frequently, such feelings do not strike a person at the outset of his or her return to a more natural way of living: it is when diet, exercise, and development of the inner faculties have been for some time on a better footing, that people begin to aspire to bringing other activities into line with their new regimen to be truly "whole" as the individuals they should be.

There can be other difficulties. Some people find there is a definite decrease in their ability in projection practices after, for instance, a visit from some particular relative or neighbor. The reason for this is usually entirely psychological, and may not be far to seek: it may well be that So-and-so is a thoroughly good sort, but that he or she is tall, or short, or thin, or fat, or fair, or dark, or something else which you feel you "never get on with." In that case, if the innocent offender doesn't come along too often, you may decide it is best just to accept the situation; and perhaps in time, by persevering with your projection practices as usual, you may very likely wear down your deep-level resistance. Or, again, you may decide that too great a hindrance to your progress is being caused by your antipathy, and you want to do something about it.

There may, again, be a different kind of psychological factor, such as that the visitor has no belief or no interest in inner development, and unfailingly brings out this negative or hostile attitude in the conversation. There is, as a matter of fact, a very direct way in which you can deal with this, or with any other type of conversation which disturbs you: DO NOT REACT. Behave just as you might if someone had just passed a particularly banal remark about the weather: make a colorless and non-committal reply, and, without undue haste, change the subject. Few people will go on being aggressive about their opinions for long in monologue, particularly if you change the subject to one in which you know that the speaker has a *positive* interest. All the same, the skepticism of a close associate might in some cases shake either your confidence or your nerves to a point where you feel you need some inner reinforcement; in which case the method of dealing with lower-self problems that is going to be given shortly, will certainly help you.

Before coming to it, however, one more type of interpersonal difficulty has to be mentioned, because it calls for quite a different treatment. You have increased and activated your energy at both physical and psychic levels; you have regulated your life in a way that should mean you are at a distinctly above-average level of health and vitality. And you need this energy, health and vitality for the new practices and experiments in astral projection that you are undertaking.

It is entirely possible you may find there is some certain person who is sometimes in your company, perhaps frequently, perhaps seldom, who causes you to feel afterwards "depleted," reduced in energy and maybe even unwilling to exert yourself to your normal extent. You will probably, on consideration, realize also that this particular person is himself or herself also "depleted" either physically or emotionally: just recovering from an illness, or suffering some disability, or having a preponderence of negative emotional attitudes: maybe depressed, desponding or apathetic. Perhaps, indeed, several people say your company "does them good." It probably does.

Now, there is no need to think of these "depleted" people as "astral vampires" or in any way "evil." It is no more "evil" for them to seek your company than for a plant to climb towards the sunlight, and what they do is probably done quite as unthinkingly. If you feel you can well spare the surplus energy—and this may be the case, *especially, if you are daily performing Formula One*—then let them have it, it can do them nothing but good. They are not "drawing energy out of you"—few people have either the will or the knowledge to do that deliberately—but energy, like water, air or any other substance capable of flowing, will find its own level and will naturally pass from those who have more to those who have less; UNLESS YOU TAKE MEASURES TO PREVENT IT.

It may very well be that at this stage in your training you may feel you can NOT spare the energy —and remember, *this decision rests entirely with you.* You are building up your available energy for specific purposes. If you goal, or one of your goals, is to help other people, you will easily perceive that you will be able to help far more people in more ways, once you are capable of consciously leaving your physical body, than is possible to you now by just passively allowing energy to be taken from you. In each separate instance YOU must decide.

If you decide not to give out your energy to the depleted, there is a very simple technique for preventing this. As an example: a young unmarried woman, physically and mentally energetic but, as a matter of fact, rather a skeptic as far as psychic matters were concerned, was stationed at the enquiries desk of a large and famous library. For long hours each day, all kinds of people came to her with their questions: the old, the young, distinguished scholars, young students, writers, teachers, folk with no place else to spend the day, cranks, derelicts, dreamers, wolves. Many people could be answered in a few words, some needed or extorted a lengthy discussion. It was exacting work anyway, but our friend was a highly qualified librarian and most of it was routine matter to her. Generally, however long the actual unraveling of an enquiry might take, she could get the drift of it in the course of the first sentence or so. Among this great cosmopolitan procession of human beings, however, there were some who never could be brought to declare any specific question, and it would dawn on her that these people—sometimes highly educated, sometimes not, and well or poorly dressed, but all *avid*—simply "wanted to talk." And, after at last getting rid of them, *she always felt exhausted*.

Although skeptical by nature, she was by no means narrow-minded, and after reflecting on the matter, she spoke about it to an occultist whom she knew well, another habitué of the great library. The advice she was given worked well, and is repeated here for any who may feel they need it:

Turn so that you do not sit quite directly facing the person, and, in meeting his gaze, concentrate only upon his *left* eye.

Cross your legs or at least your ankles, fold your arms and keep them folded if possible across your upper abdomen.

Speak slightly to one side, and, when not speaking, keep your mouth closed and your head slightly inclined forward.

This is altogether a very discreet piece of "psychic self-defense" which can easily be used in company, or in public, without any appearance of singularity. You have learned already (page 69) that for any practice connected with projection, you should NEVER cross legs or arms. Now, in this counsel as to posture for PREVENTING the flow the energy, you are told: *cross both arms and legs.* The good sense of this is doubtless apparent. You are also told not to *relate directly* to the person from whom you are defending yourself, in your bodily posture. The counsel with regard to the person's *left* eye, is so that you may not be receptive to any mental suggestion to change your posture: the *right* eye is the dominant one. If you concentrate on the left eye of the person opposite (that is, the eye facing your right eye!) you cannot easily be dominated in that way, neither can you be considered to be avoiding his gaze. The "astro-sensitive" region of the upper abdomen is also well protected.

It must be repeated that in most instances those who deplete the energy of others are doing so without deliberate intention or malice. Our friend the librarian was in a very unusual situation, where she could hardly be quite so confident of this; but the counsel just given was effective all the same.

While on this subject, it is worth noting how exactly this defense posture is contrary to the posture you would adopt if you wanted deliberately to give energy to someone. You would stand or sit squarely facing that person, at first in the Wand or the Egyptian posture, then naturally raise your arms towards him. Your gaze would be directly upon him. You would direct energy to him, either immediately from your upper abdomen or, more likely, sending it by an act of imagination along your arms to be rayed to him from your palm-centres or fingertips, perhaps with your mind formulating at the same time a general wish for his well-being or a specific thought of his recovery from whatever. A great deal of so-called "astral" or "spiritual" "healing" is done in this way, with various elaborations according to the beliefs of the practitioners; and often it is very effective, too.

The physical body has a great natural impulse towards self-healing; you don't usually have to know how to heal it, the person's own instinctual nature will take care of that part of it, but what can often be very welcome, especially after days or sickness or after the shock of an accident, is *the fresh supply of energy that you are able to provide.* You can help a great deal in this way. What you are NOT entitled to do, of course, either legally or morally, is to call yourself a healer on the strength of it. Nature heals; you, in this type of action, simply supply extra energy, although if you do have some knowledge of physiology and understanding of what is amiss you can direct that energy very specifically.

SEE NOW!—HERE IS ANOTHER OCCULT MATTER ON WHICH YOU HAVE JUST GAINED AN IMPORTANT INSIGHT, ONLY BY YOUR PRESENT UNDERSTANDING OF THE MANIPU-LATION OF ENERGY!

And what can you do for yourself? You have already been given some ways in which you can benefit your lower self—physical body, and emotional and instinctual nature—both directly and by means of the mirror image. Now you are ready for something more advanced.

You have, at this present stage in your program,

*the power to modify and adjust the relationship
between many outside factors and yourself, by means
of THE NEXT FORMULA THAT WE ARE GOING
TO CONSIDER.* It makes use only of abilities that
you have already awakened and developed if you
have been working through this book; but the use of
it, if you develop it thoughtfully according to your
particular needs,
 CAN, LITERALLY, TRANSFORM YOUR LIFE!

 Yes. THIS FORMULA CAN TRANSFORM
YOUR LIFE. Some men and women who make a cult
of the physical body, take courses of exercise and
massage which they call "body sculpture." Now you,
if you wish it, can do some "soul sculpture." The
kind of thing referred to earlier in this chapter—the
irrational craving for things you don't want to want;
the irrational aversion to people you have no cause to
dislike, the fact that some of their mannerisms
or peculiarities, or some of your own mannerisms or
peculiarities "get you down," or that some long-past
childhood trauma still undermines your self-
confidence—these things are all in your power to
work on. You can put it all behind you. *You can't
change other people, but you CAN change your
reaction to them!*

 Don't, however, mistake the purpose of this. An
occult technique is NOT the right answer (except as a

very last resort) if——

Your projection practice is disturbed by your neighbor's over-loud TV or radio; or

A meal-time that has been fixed for you makes it impossible; or

You can't get away from the family for a session by yourself, even by locking yourself in the bathroom;

Or any other difficulty of this order.

Human beings—especially quiet, reserved and studious-minded human beings—are sometimes apt to forget one very obvious fact:

THE NORMAL FIRST STEP TOWARDS GETTING ANYTHING YOU WANT IN THIS WORLD, IS TO ASK FOR IT.

If what you want is likely to make difficulties for other people, of course try to think of some way this can either be avoided or compensated. If, for instance, it might mean asking a busy housewife to cook a separate meal for you, then offer either to cook it yourself, or to do her shopping (or something else as the case may be). Anyway, COMMUNICATE. It's all part of that give-and-take of energies which is so good for you, not only within your own psyche but at interpersonal levels as well; and besides, people being what they are (rather unperceptive, but not ogres) you most probably will get what you ask for, be it peace and quiet or anything else.

You may have read of the great claims made—

legitimately in many cases—for the possibilities of new happiness that can be gained from various forms of autogenic treatment or self-hypnosis. Different methods are employed to relax the body and to stop ingrained habits of thought or of emotion from intervening, so that the subject can get some good advice of his own choosing home to his deeper emotional and instinctual levels. YOU DON'T NEED THAT TYPE OF TECHNIQUE. WITH THE KNOWLEDGE YOU ALREADY HAVE, A METHOD IS AT YOUR DISPOSAL FOR ACHIEVING THE SAME RESULTS—INDEED, EVEN MORE FAR-REACHING RESULTS—WITH NO FURTHER PRELIMINARIES, NO HYPNOSIS.

If any inner problem is hindering your projection program, be the problem an old one or new, reflect on it, try to see its roots as clearly as you can, and then go to work on it.

FORMULA THREE

The Simulacrum.

(To be performed in your chosen Projection Area.)

Stand upright in the Wand Posture, establish the Rhythmic Breath.

Perform Formula One.

Spend a short time in reflection on the relationship between your rational mind and your Higher
Self. *(Your rational mind tends to consider everything in the light of reason, but sometimes the Higher
Self prompts an idea or an action which springs from
something higher than reason. If you don't feel you
have ever consciously experienced this, that's all
right; what you have to do is to recognize that this
could happen, and, that if it did happen, the right
response for your rational mind would be to go along
with it: just as your rational mind expects your
emotional nature to go along with* it.*)* Have a
deliberate intention, at this present time, that your
rational mind and your Higher Self should be in
harmony and should be working together; this will
give a special authority and rightness to your
decisions which will be uttered in this Formula.

In your visual imagination, exteriorize astral
substance from the region of your upper abdomen.
Some ten feet from you, form it first into a misty
cloud and then into a simulacrum, as close a likeness
of yourself as possible, standing facing towards you.

*(This simulacrum represents your Lower Self,
partly by being a likeness of your physical appearance,
as with the mirror image. The simulacrum is far more
than a mirror image, however, because it is part of
the living substance of your astral body, and is
intimately related to your emotional and instinctual
nature; it is a true representative of your lower
nature.)*

Speak to the simulacrum. Greet it, then address it
with gentle authority and concern. Speak to it from
the joint seniority of your rational mind and Higher
Self combined, with all the love and reassurance you
can express. *(You may, if you feel moved to do so,
address it as your child [according to the teachings of
occult philosophy, your lower self and your physical
body are indeed "offspring" of your Higher Self],
but you may be happier to consider it as a younger
brother or sister. In any case, you—your rational
mind guided by your Higher Self—have the inalienable
responsibility of decision-making for the happiness
and right fulfillment of this irrational, sensitive and
wayward being. Therefore, speak firmly but with
sincere love and tenderness. Don't rush; don't try to
cover overmany subjects, and above all don't go in for
long abstract reasonings. At the same time, this is no
place for the encapsuled triteness of the hypnotist's
customary technique. It is of no use telling this
representative of your lower self, "You are happy and*

*at peace," if your lower self has been silently
burdened for years with some childhood anguish, or
is fearful now that you'll give up the drink which it,
as a possible example, secretly identifies [unsuspected
by your rational mind] with strength and manhood.
You should speak at more length: something like,
for instance, "I know you have been unhappy, but
the cause of that is past. You are capable, you are
strong, your instincts are good and natural. You and
I together are even stronger, and, under the direction
of our Higher Self, we are bound for the heights."
Add any specific facts or directions you know to be
appropriate; as you continue to use this Formula,
and also the tape-teaching method still to be
described in this chapter, you may discover further
points on which you can be quite exact.)* Everything
in this part of the procedure should be uttered
LOVINGLY.

Now, you should thank your lower self for
helping you in this action; it is appropriate also to
give it a blessing, which might suitably be in the name
of your Higher Self, or the Divine Spark within you.

The next step is to re-absorb the Simulacrum.

This done, state aloud once more *(but in some-*

what briefer form) the resolutions or counsel which in this session you enjoined upon the Simulacrum.

Again perform Formula One.

(This concludes Formula Three. All that you have said to the Simulacrum will now be assimilated by your entire Lower Self.)
Even if you have no problems whatever such as have been instanced in this chapter, you should, none the less, use Formula Three from time to time with a suitable and more general address to the lower self. Not only is it an excellent way of maintaining communication with the lower self: perhaps even more important is the function of this Formula in keeping the rational mind aware of its responsibility and of its right relation to the Higher Self. It is the same within the levels of the psyche as in human affairs: we must accept responsibility for those less mature or less capable of organizing their own life effectively, but we can only exercise this responsibility aright if the reasoning mind accepts in its turn the guidance of a higher authority than itself. Otherwise, the saying *"Power corrupts"* can be as true of the ego in its station of authority over the lower faculties, as when it has been said of any dictator in history.

One observation that can be made about this Formula of the Simulacrum, is that *it allows the lower self no opportunity to reply to the admonitions that are given to it.* When the Simulacrum has been re-absorbed we do not wait, as we do after re-absorbing the Watcher, for its impressions to rise into our conscious mind.

In just the same way, and for just the same reason, a doctor doesn't treat a vaccination sore in the same way that he treats a boil. He, in the case of the vaccination—and you, in the case of the Simulacrum—intend the "dosage" to stay inside.

But the lower self may need to "dialogue" its education?

It may very validly have such a need, and we shall also learn how better to help it if we allow it to reply for itself. However, it must be remembered that the natural language of the lower self is not really expressed in words but in symbols; for this reason it can express itself most clearly while we sleep, while our consciousness is receptive to the imagery of dreams. Only occasionally will it manifest itself in the verbal language of daytime, in the kind of lapse the psychologists delight in recording: "Ah, your big occasion!—I do indeed look forward to being absent!" The dream world is its proper territory.

For this reason, if you are re-educating your lower self in any significant manner, it is very desirable to take two further measures. One is, *to make a tape, in which you will say over again the points you want your lower self to assimilate.* The other is, *to keep a diary of your dreams.*

The tape is to be played over, not while you are asleep, but *while you are going to sleep.* The ideal advice would be, to tell you to recapitulate mentally your directions to your lower self, while dozing off at night; but the mind is so apt to wander at such a time, *and the lower self, the intended recipient itself, is so apt to intervene and make you say something you didn't intend,* that you are much safer with the correct message on tape. Plan the recording carefully, in short elementary sentences—you aren't talking to your intellect—and with as much repetition as will go on a 45-minute tape (C-90). Record it in a clear but soft, gentle and kindly voice. If it is soothing enough to lull you to sleep, so much the better.

This tape should, naturally, be re-made from time to time as the requirements change. Take care, however, to keep the written record of each text, with the dates of first and last using; this will make an important supplement to your dream diary.

With regard to the dream diary, you may be surprised (especially if you are a person who usually is not very conscious of dreaming) how your dreams will seem to intensify both in meaningfulness and in vividness as soon as they are "encouraged" by your attention. The knack is to keep a scribble-pad and pencil beside your bed, with a workable lamp for night use, so that immediately on awaking you can note down any remembered dream. A good plan is to outline it in a few words at first, then to go back and fill in all possible detail. Don't at this stage worry about literary form, just get every possible fact: and, of course don't attempt to rationalize. Later in the day, re-read this rough account. See if upon reflection any further detail or interpretation occurs to you, then write the dream in the dream diary: a straight account of the dream in the first person (*"I was standing by the sea . . ."*) and *then* any notes which you want to add. Add illustrations, if you feel like it.

You will learn much. You may perhaps see thin Miss X., who gives you the jitters despite her friendly smile, turn before your eyes into a bad-tempered schoolteacher you forgot (or seemed to have forgotten) years back. If you are telling your lower self to be brisk and punctual, it may answer you with a dream clearly based on the old story about the tortoise who won the race against the hare. This gives you something to think about: is your lower self really putting you right about something—it could be—or is this just a particular tale that over-impressed you as a child? Or you may see a muddy pool change into a clear spring of fresh water, and know this to be a true message representing a hidden problem you've now cleared up. Or you may dream of being offered now a car, now a boat, now an aeroplane, now a caravan—and you may think of your projection program and say to yourself, "True, very true, I'll be taking off soon now!"

As a fact, you probably will from time to time dream of your projection program. You may even have dreams which seem plainly to be more than dreams, which indicate that the astral "limbering-up" process you have undertaken has already induced spontaneous out-of-the-body experience. If this happens, it's good and encouraging. You will not be inclined to dismiss it as phantasy, now, as you might perhaps have done at one time. Your rational mind now knows that astral journeying is a reality.

All the same, persevere. You are coming to the main objective of this book, the goal of your painstaking practices and of so many fascinating experimentations: the achievement of WILLED AND DELIBERATE ASTRAL PROJECTION, IN FULL CONSCIOUSNESS, AND TO YOUR OWN PLANNED TIME AND PURPOSE.

The Formula of the Simulacrum should be used daily for at least two weeks, Formula Two not being practiced at that time; then use either Two or Three at will. If *neither* is being used for some reason, then you should follow the directions given at the end of Chapter 4 for use of Formula One with or without Exteriorization of Astral Substance.

THE DREAM DIARY

On the next page is a suggested layout for facing pages of the Dream Diary, for use in conjunction with Formula Three and the bed-time tape. It provides for the need to perceive any response that may occur in dreams to the previous day's messages to the unconscious mind.

The student is urged to note the day of the week as well as the date, because patterns of association for particular days often reveal hidden emotional contents.

Day and date _____ *

FORMULA THREE
Salient points of message given today to Simulacrum.

THE BEDTIME TAPE
If a new one is instituted this evening, give its salient points; otherwise state "As before."

Day and date _____ *

DREAMS

ASSOCIATED IDEAS, PROBABLE INTERPRETATION

*Dreams being recorded the day after dreaming, the date on the right-hand page should be the day after the date on the left.

Check Point

5

• *FORMULA THREE, THE FORMULA OF THE SIMULACRUM has great value in dealing with "problems" as you may desire, but should, in any case, be used regularly at this stage in the program, for its value in knitting together the* Three Levels of the Psyche: *the* Higher Self, Rational Mind, *and* Lower Self.

• *Formula Three contains use of Formula One, Exteriorization of Astral Substance, shaping it, sending it to a distance, recalling it, reabsorbing it, collecting impressions from it. Postures: Wand and Egyptian.*

• *In connection with this Formula, the MAKING*

149

OF A TAPE for use while going to sleep is recommended, and the KEEPING OF A DREAM DIARY.

• *This chapter also gives procedures you can use as and when you wish: TO AVOID DEPLETION OF ENERGY, and TO GIVE ENERGY AT WILL.*

• Keep up the HEALTH DIET and PHYSICAL EXERCISE. Keep using FORMULA ONE at all times!

Soul Sculpture

Personal Notes

Soul Sculpture

Study Points

6

Willed, Fully Conscious, Astral Projection.

1. When your Dream Diary shows some "projection-type" dreams, program a new going-to-
   sleep tape:
   a. To gain control over sleep-projections.
   b. To give the Lower Self instructions to follow
      during such sleep-projections.
   c. To make the return from projection to the
      physical body smoothly and easily.
2. Don't confuse dream-projections with true
   conscious astral projection!
3. Practice for the Imaginary Projection of Consciousness:
   a. With the aid of a plant, aquarium or picture,

enter into a visible scene.

b. Adapt your imagined presence to a size and condition suited to the scene.

c. Act within the scene, as if you were an actor in a play—only make it more real than any play: feel elements of the scene upon your skin, hear sounds, smell, move, etc.

d. Return to normal consciousness feeling relaxed and refreshed. You have been on vacation!

4. The Imagination works upon, and through, the Astral Body. The above exercise gives your Lower Self practice in handling data separate from that normally transmitted through the physical body's neural system.

5. Locate your Centre of Consciousness: where, in your physical body, does your sense of personality attach?

6. *Formula Four—Willed Projection of Consciousness:*

a. Assume the Earth Posture.

b. Perform Formula One.

c. Send forth to a convenient distance above you a jet of silver-grey mist.

d. Form it into a key-figure, in the same posture as yourself, facing you. **Note:** do not form it as the Simulacrum!

e. Intensify your awareness of selfhood at your Centre of Consciousness to a single point.

f. Mentally determine to transfer yourself to

the key-figure.

g. Imagine that you, concentrated into that single point of consciousness as in "e" above, are gliding swiftly upward towards the key-figure, and entering it at the point corresponding to your own Centre of Consciousness.

h. Now, "turn around" within the key-figure and see the room from its viewpoint—see your physical body below, facing you.

i. "Feel yourself into" the astral vehicle (the key-figure)—locate your hands, feet, etc.

7. Return from the astral vehicle:

a. Turn around (turn the astral vehicle you now inhabit) so that you are facing upwards in the Earth Posture, about eight feet above your physical body.

b. Renew your awareness of the astral vehilcle.

c. Sink, in your astral vehicle, slowly downward into your physical body.

d. Feel a renewed sensory awareness of your physical body.

8. If, at this time, you find you are not making rapid progress in achieving full astral projection, check back over the program for problem-areas. *There is absolutely no reason why you cannot succeed!* The most frequent problem areas are physical lethargy and mental negation.

a. Diet and exercise should be kept at a personal optimum. Indulgences in alcohol and

tobacco may have to be reduced, or elimi-
nated, for some people.
b. Discipline may be needed. The program with
its repetition of practices is important.
c. Mental negation: your rational mind may
still deny the reality of projection—influ-
enced by fear or even by love—as in the case
of someone dear to you not approving of
your astral projection work. The Formula of
the Simulacrum must be used to lead the
Lower Self gently into a more self-confident
and spontaneous attitude.
9. Some people may like to have material aids in
their astral projection work. These are used as a
kind of "code" to the Lower Self.
a. Before assuming the Earth Posture, a trace
of Oil of Jasmine can be applied to the forehead between the eyebrows—the "Third
Eye" area.
b. Or you can burn an incense compounded of
Mastic Gum, Oil of Jasmine and powdered
Orris Root.
c. Absolute regularity of the routine—the time
and place, clothing, etc.—also acts as a
"code" alerting the Lower Self.

OUT OF THE BODY!

You have now had a fair amount of experience, of one sort and another, of exteriorizing astral substance. You are accustomed to using the FORMULA OF THE SIMULACRUM, and once any initial personal obstacles have been smoothed out by the use of this, you have this valuable formula for use freely in educating the different levels of your psyche to work together in a harmonious partnership. This you can at every step direct so as to make it *helpful in your program for out-of-the-body experience*; so that in this, as in everything else, you will find that *what is helpful for your general bodily and psychic well-being, is good also for your astral projection program.*

You are also accustomed to using the FORMULA OF THE WATCHER, so that you know by experience that a shape of astral substance can travel away from your pnysical body, is capable of sensory perceptions, and can be recalled without difficulty. By the verification of impressions brought back by the Watcher, furthermore, you will have been able to assure yourself of the reality of the astral shape and of its journeys.

You should, if your DREAM DIARY is showing up any "projection-type" dreams (it probably is, now and then) give yourself a new going-to-sleep tape, containing something on these lines:

IF I TRAVEL OUT FROM MY BODY DURING SLEEP, I WILL TAKE DELIBERATE CONTROL OF THE SITUATION.

IF I AM NAKED, I WILL CLOTHE MYSELF IN ASTRAL GARMENTS.

IF I AM FLYING, I WILL DETERMINE MY DIRECTION AND MY LANDING PLACE.

IF I MEET OTHER PERSONS, I WILL TEACH AND ASSIST THOSE WHO NEED IT, AND WILL TRY TO LEARN FROM THOSE WHO ARE WISER THAN I AM.

The exact words must of course depend upon your own needs. To dream of being without clothing, to meet with other people and to be so disconcerted as to speed from their company or (quite frequently) to wake up with a jump, is a fairly common sign of involuntary astral projection. The lower consciousness, until it is very well trained, in forming a vehicle for itself naturally tends to forget such a refinement as clothing. The lower consciousness, after all, is what you came into the world with; but then, upon encounter with other entities, a more mature social awareness asserts itself. The peculiar "jump" of awakening is another sign, a sudden jerking back of astral substance into the body. If the sleeper can consciously take control of the situation, this can be avoided.

Training oneself to become aware of an astral projection during sleep, that is, asserting the rational mind to direct what might otherwise be an aimless and merely instinctual wandering, is good practice. *It still must not be confused, however, with the true object of your endeavors, that is, THE WILLED GOING FORTH IN FULL CONSCIOUSNESS IN A DELIBERATELY-FORMED ASTRAL VEHICLE, THE PERFORMANCE OF AN INTENDED SERIES OF ACTS WHILE IN PROJECTION, AND THE SUBSEQUENT WILLED RETURN TO THE PHYSICAL BODY.*

Imaginary Projection of Consciousness

Just as at other stages of this program you have begun by carrying out in imagination something which you afterwards perform in fact, now you are going to give yourself some practice in the imaginary projection of consciousness. This experience also will have value in everyday life, for on occasions when you have neither time nor need to project an astral vehicle for yourself, it can be very restful and relaxing to detach yourself for a few minutes from your physical body by sending your consciousness imaginatively into a situation of pleasant adventure or of repose.

Everyone does this to a very minor extent all the time, without even thinking about it. Why else are we accustomed to hang on our walls pictures of pleasant scenes, landscapes, attractive human forms, or animals with which we feel some particular affinity? Or, simply, with pictures of our friends?

Surely it is in every case so that among the day's occupations or on awaking in the morning, the eye can dwell upon something or someone in whose presence the consciousness loves to linger, be it with the smile on a loved face; the serenity of earth, sky or water; the beauty and suggested excitement of a ship, or the lithe muscles and sleek coat of a living creature.

A picture, preferably a landscape, can very well be utilized for practice in separating the consciousness from the body, but as a first example let us consider something else that may be in your home, a potted plant (perhaps one which shows a fair amount of earth at the base of the main stem, not overhanging it entirely with leaves) or a tank of tropical fish, preferably with aquatic plants and perhaps a rock or so. It is a pleasure to look at these fragments of the natural world existing in our homes,

BUT NOW YOU ARE GOING TO DO MUCH MORE THAN JUST LOOK.

The Plant. Sit comfortably near your plant, if possible so that the rim of the pot is just below eye level. The consciousness is in no way limited to the dimensions of the physical body, so as you let your gaze travel slowly up the stem you can imagine it to be a huge tropical or prehistoric tree. Imagine yourself standing just within the rim of the pot; you go forward carefully over the huge earth-granules or rocks, and you reach your tree. You can, if you like, sit down at the foot of it and gaze up into the foliage; or perhaps you would like to climb upward among the branches. You can make your way from branch to branch, or you can stretch along a stem, up there among the leaves. Or perhaps you prefer to fly like a bird into the branches and settle there; or, if your plant has blossoms, to explore these in the manner of a bee or a humming-bird. Whatever you do, rest there a little while, really savoring and enjoying this new experience; be aware of yourself in that setting, feel the leaves and flowers around you, or the fern-fronds. If should make a little vacation for your consciousness. When you return from it, come back the way you went; once again, the abrupt transition is to be avoided. Bring back a memory with you, of coolness, peace and beauty and, maybe, of a sweet mossy or floral fragrance.

The Aquarium. Another time, sit beside your tank of tropical fish. There's no need to make your field of consciousness so small that the guppies look like White Sharks, but imagine yourself about the size of a fairly small fish—one which is able to dart through the water of the tank or to bask in the green shade of the water-plants. Then feel, harmlessly brushing your side, the smooth armor of a companion. Gaze into a watchful gold-and-black eye that gazes back at you without expression but in total alertness. Sense in your own being how the owner of that eye feels: peaceful, unworried, yet with every fin poised and ready for an instant change of direction. Join in the sudden spontaneous dance of the two or three who are seized with an impulsive ecstasy of swirling rhythmic movement; then glide,

glide ... Again, dwell for a time in this extension of consciousness, and return soothed and refreshed.

The Picture. Now, you should be able to act similarly with a two-dimensional scene, a picture. If this is a landscape, the simplest plan is for you to see it as natural size, with yourself as a human being—*but don't "see" yourself, of course*—who will walk into that field; cross that stream or maybe wade up it; sit on that wall or under that tree; climb that hill and contemplate a further view from the summit ... Your imagination, aided by data from all the natural scenery you have every explored, should be able to fill in the feel of the breeze on your skin, the calling of birds, the smell of grass and wild plants under the sun.

This evocation of different sense-data, in a way which depends entirely upon the imagination, has considerable importance: *the imagination works upon, and through, the astral body.* Your instinctual lower self is habitually concerned in handling sense-data brought in from the material world by the neural system, but it has little practice, outside of dreams, in processing data apart from the neural system. By means of the imaginative practices, your astral body and its substance will become accustomed to employ not only the faculty of sight, but the faculties of other senses as well. On the other hand, each one of these practices, intended to produce effects in the imagination, has peculiarities which should clearly distinguish its results from those of genuine projection in an astral vehicle.

WITHOUT ANY DOUBT, YOU WILL KNOW WHEN YOU DO THE "REAL THING." IT IS DIFFERENT FROM DREAM, DIFFERENT FROM ANY "MAKE-BELIEVE" USE OF THE IMAGINA- TION, HOWEVER VIVID. YOU WILL KNOW THAT YOU ARE FULLY AWAKE. Nevertheless, the *quality* of what you will do then can be improved by what you do do now, just as a preliminary practicing of the strokes on dry land can help a learner to become a better swimmer, and just as a child playing at some skill that attracts it will come to it better prepared, as an adolescent, than would a boy or girl who had never thought of it before.

From these imaginative practices, then, you will learn that your consciousness can immerse itself in an activity which does not involve the physical body, even though in the examples given there is physical sense-data present as a series of guiding stimuli; and the faculties of sight, hearing, touch, smell and taste can have a reality for you quite apart from any employment of the physical senses. *You may find that the results of these imaginary sensory games will be reflected in the contents of your dream diary.*

Some people only dream in black and white, some never dream about hearing sounds of any sort; to dream of a smell or a flavor is quite uncommon. Textures, and the feeling of contact of one sort or another are, however, not infrequent. Do you find color, music, perhaps even perfumes, coming more into your dreams now? That's exciting!

While you explore these matters, however, your use of Formula Two or Three, or, at the least, of Formula One, should continue as in the previous directions.

Your Centre of Consciousness

One more question remains to be answered, and nobody but yourself can determine the right answer in your particular case:

When you are in normal consciousness, wide awake in your physical body, and something calls for a special effort from YOU PERSONALLY, to what point in your body does your sense of individual personality seem to attach?

Or, to put it differently, *When you say "I myself" what seems to you to be the location of "I"?*

This varies from one person to another, but it probably will be one of the following: forehead, eyes, throat, solar plexus. Furthermore, this question does *not* have to be decided "once and for all." You may, after some experimentation, decide your first decision was not the right one; or you may feel it was right to begin with, but as time has passed a change has taken place and, with progressive development, your centre of consciousness has shifted. Such a possibility is altogether valid and reasonable; all that is required is that you should keep an awareness of what is, for you, the right answer at any given time.

FORMULA FOUR

Willed Projection of Consciousness

(To be performed in your chosen Projection Area.)

Lie down in the Earth Posture. *(You will notice that this practice is performed in a different posture from the previous ones, which all call for a standing or sitting position.)*

Free of physical limitations.

Perform Formula One. *(Do this exactly as if you were standing; for instance, the "fountain of light" at the end of the procedure will travel horizontally from your insteps to your head, will divide just beyond your crown and will pass outside your arms to your feet again.)*

Now send forth to a convenient distance above you a jet of silver-grey mist. It should form at that distance into a small cloud; under pressure of sustained ejection it should increase rapidly in size, and should become more defined until it takes on your own size and general shape. You should fashion it as the "Key Figure" described previously (page 102), and in the same posture as yourself, but facing you. *(That is to say, it will be floating in the air above you, in a horizontal position, looking down at you; but it should NOT be an exact replica of you like "The Simulacrum," it will be the much simplified version called the "Key Figure.")*

Keep clearly in visualization this projection figure and its connecting cord, and, while doing so, intensify your awareness of selfhood at your especial "Centre of Consciousness." Continue until you have a distinct, vital and glowing sense of "presence" at that particular point.

Then be aware of the corresponding point on the Key Figure.

Make a single clear resolution (*mentally, not aloud*) to transfer yourself to that astral vehicle. Directly you have made this resolution, imagine yourself, concentrated as it were in your single point of consciousness, gliding swiftly upwards towards the figure and entering it at the point corresponding to your own Centre of Consciousness.

Now make a deliberate mental effort to "turn around" in the figure, so as to see from its viewpoint. *("See" the room as from somewhere near the ceiling—and include your own physical body lying below you, facing up towards you.)*

THIS CHANGE OF PERSPECTIVE IS THE CRITICAL POINT TO SECURE A TRUE TRANSFER OF CONSCIOUS-NESS. Having achieved this transfer, you will have, as it were, to "feel yourself into" the vehicle: locate your feet, hands and so on. *(This is difficult to describe; it is rather like putting on a thick glove, but also it is like awaking from a heavy sleep and renewing awareness of your body.)*

THE FIRST TIME YOU SUCCEED IN TRANSFERING CONSCIOUSNESS, DON'T ATTEMPT MUCH MORE THAN THIS!

AFTER MAKING A SUCCESSFUL TRANSFER OF CONSCIOUSNESS, the return presents no difficulty. *In theory,* you—your astral presence—should lie full length facing upward about eight feet directly above your physical body; you should renew your awareness of the astral vehicle (*so as to be conscious of taking it with you*), and you should then sink down slowly, by an act of will, towards and into your physical body. After a brief interval, you should be aware of renewed sensory consciousness of your physical body—again, as if awakening from sleep. *In practice,* at least for some time, as soon as you draw near to your physical body you will find yourself spontaneously reunited with it.

That is the formula; but you may not succeed at the first attempt. It is the change of perspective, the "turn around," that really secures success. You can continue trying to align yourself with the astral vehicle in order to achieve this, but on no account should you go on trying when the necessary concentration is causing fatigue. In the next practice session, proceed with equal care and benefit by your increased experience.

Some people do succeed at the first attempt, some need more, but your program helps. *Always the various Formulae should be continued meanwhile, so that your endeavors will be balanced, healthy and vital.* When you do succeed, the new viewpoint may be realized so naturally and easily that it takes a moment or two to comprehend what has happened; or it may be accompanied by the "metallic click" which is its traditional sign.

When you have succeeded, be content for the first few times to look around, to come down from your floating position, to move about the room. At this stage you will probably be happiest to "walk" in earthly fashion. DON'T GO TOO NEAR YOUR PHYSICAL BODY UNTIL YOU MEAN TO RETURN, OR YOU MAY "SNAP BACK" INTO IT INADVERTENTLY. BUT, ALSO, DON'T STAY "OUT" FOR TOO LONG. Especially if your sense of hearing is somewhat lacking at first—as it well may be—there is a dreadful sense of solitude in out-of-the-body experience that can descend with a sudden feeling of panic. One usual result of this is that it drives people, before they have the necessary experience and power of co-ordination, to travel forth and to try to make their presence known to a friend. The result can be a nasty fright for the friend if you succeed, and considerable bewilderment and maybe exhaustion for yourself if you fail. And so take it easy until you are sure of your astral faculties. *Remember—your astral vehicle is made of substance which, of its very nature, responds more swiftly to an emotional impulse than to a rational direction.* It needs training, and you need practice in directing it.

One thing you need to know at the outset is how to conclude any practice session when, for whatever reason, having exteriorized astral substance you DON'T transfer your consciousness to the astral vehicle.

IN THAT CASE, YOU *MUST* RE-ASSIMILATE THE SUBSTANCE THAT YOU HAVE EXTERIOR-IZED. If you have formed it into the Key Figure, turn it back into a smoky cloud, and then go on to re-assimilate the cloud—*as in the other formulae.*

There is one exception to this rule. If, after ejecting astral substance—whether you get as far as shaping the Key Figure or not—you fail to complete your intended practice BECAUSE YOU FALL ASLEEP, there is no need when you awake to reabsorb any astral substance, because you will have done so instinctively during sleep.

This is true of astral substance exteriorized in the course of any practice given in this book, but it is given mention especially here because the lying-down Earth Posture assumed for Formula Four makes it rather more frequent for people to fall asleep during this practice than during any other.

If you DO transfer your consciousness to the astral vehicle, even if only for a brief while, there is of course no need to re-assimilate astral substance, because *when you return to the body you bring the astral vehicle back with you.* This is true, whether you succeed in making your return with full deliberation or whether you simply "snap back."

IN ANY CASE, after a re-assimilation, or if you have any doubts, or if after a "snap back" (waking or sleeping) you feel a bit "blurred at the edges," there is a ready aid at hand which CAN DO YOU NOTHING BUT GOOD, whatever the circumstances. Do a "FORMULA ONE."

It is strongly recommended that Formula Four, like all the other practices involving ejection of astral substance, should be performed in the most loose and easy of garments, or in no garments at all. This lack of any constriction will greatly facilitate reabsorption.

FORMULA FOUR represents a method of astral projection which has brought *rapid success* to a very large number of men and women. Anyone who does not succeed as soon as he or she expects should *check back over the program* to see where reinforcement may be needed. The most frequent problem areas are *physical lethargy* and *mental negation*. The means of combating both these are provided within this program. Diet and physical exercise should be kept at the personal optimum; also it is a fact, as is pointed out on page 127, that for some people ANY indulgence in alcohol or tobacco is too much. (For rather complex reasons of body chemistry, this is more frequently the case with vegetarians than with meat-eaters; but though this means that in some ways the vegetarians have to take extra care, it also means they gain more, health-wise, in the long run!)

As for mental negation: if, after first-hand experience of the reality of astral substance, its ejection and control, anyone's rational mind is still trying to deny the evidence (*and we know this can happen, from the very usual reaction of so-called "scientific" minds towards valid evidence which would overthrow an established hypothesis*) then the treatment should be with the Formula of the Simulacrum.

How is that, when the Formula of the Simulacrum is to re-educate the lower self? The lower self is emotional and instinctual; the problem here is a matter of reason.

Don't be deceived! Can the reasoning faculty deny reason? The most logical of reasoning can go astray, if its logic begins from one false premise; *and the data from which most people begin their reasoning is dictated, at least in part, by emotional promptings.* To a great extent, this is what makes us human beings instead of computerized robots, but we do have to be on our guard to see that this habit of reasoning from emotionally-selected "facts" does not trap us into attitudes which we shall regret.

So, anyone who, after experiencing personally that astral projection IS SO, still finds his or her "rational mind" insisting that it CAN'T BE SO, should *not* go on trying to cudgel that mind with logic, but should take a look behind the scenes.

What is the emotion involved?—love or fear?

It will be one or the other. A parent, grandparent or other relative, or a teacher at whatever level—someone greatly loved or greatly feared—will have implanted the idea that astral or psychic experience "doesn't happen," and the victim of love or of fear goes on trying to maintain, even in the face of experience, that it "doesn't happen." Such a person may indeed FORBID anything of the sort to happen. Or again, a person may cling, either with a loving sense of loyalty or with a fear-motivated obedience, to a notion that the development of our natural psychic faculties is somehow "wicked" regardless of the way it appears to the personal reasoning powers. In all these cases, it is the *lower self* that needs to be gently led, by means of the Formula of the Simulacrum, into a more self-confident and spontaneous attitude.

Some people, however, of a more frankly emotional, sensuous or ritualistic temperament, may welcome a more considerable build-up on the material level to accompany their practices in astral projection. For such temperaments, material aids can be of great assistance in the formation of habits of practice: a certain smell, or a certain sound, can be established as a code with the instinctual level of the psyche (again, this can very well be facilitated by explaining it in a simple way to the Simulacrum) to mean that the hour has come for the day's practice in astral projection, or for out-of-the-body experience. *(These aids are not essential, and they ought never to be considered as essential, but they can communicate very swiftly with the lower self.)* If it is desired to burn an incense, a compound of mastic gum, oil of jasmine, and powdered orris root makes a suitable blend; or, before assuming the Earth Posture, a trace of oil of jasmine can be applied to the forehead. This particular fragrance has a tradition of use for that purpose.

In any case, whatever else may be done, the best plan for astral projection is to establish as far as possible an absolute regularity of routine. The lower self is a creature of habit, of tradition and of precedent. Go along with it in this, and it will do much for you.

Check Point

6

- *Initially, you are using Formula Three, keeping a Dream Diary, and using a Bedtime Tape. Alternatively to Formula Three (after the first two weeks), you can from time to time use Formula Two as you may wish. If any cause prevents the use of Formula Two and Formula Three, then Formula One, with or without the Ejection of Astral Substance practice according to circumstances, is used. THIS ROUTINE HOLDS GOOD UNTIL YOU SUCCEED WITH FORMULA FOUR.*

Along with the above, *you now*:
- *Give yourself A NEW TAPE, as suggested in the text.*
- *Practice IMAGINARY PROJECTION OF CONSCIOUSNESS.*
- *Find YOUR CENTRE OF CONSCIOUSNESS.*

• When you are ready, *proceed to FORMULA FOUR. This contains Earth Posture, Formula One, Exteriorization of Astral Substance, Formation of the Key Figure, and* PROJECTION OF CONSCIOUS-NESS INTO THE ASTRAL VEHICLE. *Note also the* Technique for the Return.

• *If not successful, REMEMBER TO RE-ABSORB ASTRAL SUBSTANCE. REVIEW DIET AND DAILY PROGRAM. REVIEW (AND IF NECESSAY RE-PROGRAM) WORK WITH THE SIMULACRUM. BE PATIENT AND PERSEVERING.*

• AFTER SUCCESS, KEEP LIFE STYLE AND ASTRAL PRACTICES: ABOVE ALL, FORMULA ONE. *MORE ADVENTURE AWAITS YOU!*

Out of the Body

Personal Notes

Out of the Body

Study Points

7

Opportunities in Astral Projection:

1. By developing your astral faculties, you can improve the use of the corresponding faculties of the physical body—sight, hearing, etc.
2. By working with and upon the astral body, you can work upon the physical body, and also establish emotional/energy patterns that can result in self-improvement.
3. During astral projection, you can "will" astral substance along the cord from the physical body to the astral vehicle, and vice versa:
   a. More astral substance to the astral vehicle brings you closer to the earth level for the transfer of energy as in healing, or for com-

munication with in-the-body people.

   b. Less astral substance to the astral vehicle enables you to rise to higher levels of the astral world.

4. By visiting a person or place of concern to you in the astral, and then rising to higher levels while still relating to the same scene, you gain more knowledge from "behind the scenes."

5. Astral travel for two is possible.

   a. You can help another person in his or her projection.

   b. You can visit another person.

   c. You can travel and experience together.

6. Astral Sex is rapture!

   a. While in the astral, you can visit another person still in the physical body.

   b. A woman in the astral can take substance from a man in the physical, and come into very close contact with him, and experience sexual pleasure.

   c. A man in the astral is more limited, and cannot—while in the astral—experience an orgasm with a physical partner, as can a woman. But he can, like the woman, visit and experience a great deal of emotional pleasure.

   d. A man and woman both able to project can, however, meet in their astral bodies and enjoy much greater pleasure than is possible in purely physical sex. They can merge completely together, "burning as a single flame;" they can experience delight in any area of the body; they can make fantasies become "real" shared experiences; and they can experience more in the way of union without the limitation of the physical.

e. There are purely astral opportunities— including the Astral Kiss.

f. Astral sex can clarify the physical relationship—opening areas of communication limited in the physical, and through such things as fantasy-play relieve tensions that inhibit them at physical levels.

ADVENTURE IN THE ASTRAL WORLDS

7

So now you've mastered the knack of going in full consciousness out from your physical body, and into your astral vehicle. Obviously you don't want to spend any more time than is strictly necessary in looking down on your unconscious physical body or in practicing moving around your projection area.

What Is the Next Step?

The next step may very well be to go in your own consciousness to wherever you may habitually have sent a Watcher. The reason for this is that your lower

self (and therefore your astral vehicle) will already
have a distinct idea of the journey there and back;
also, from impressions brought back by your Watcher,
you will have some feeling of what that place is like
from an astral viewpoint. This can be in some ways
different from a material viewpoint. You may find,
for instance, that you are seeing material objects in
something very like the so-called "reversed perspective" which is common to traditional Oriental and
"primitive" European paintings: that is, you are
seeing rather more round the sides of the object than
you would in normal physical perspective. The
reasons for this are complex, depending partly on the
nature of the astral world, and partly on the nature
of your astral vehicle whose "seeing power" is only
partly limited by your bodily habit but in fact is
capable of giving you a much wider range of vision.

Indeed, you may discover, perhaps rather discon-
certingly, that you can sometimes see "out of the
back of your head" in your astral vehicle. You may
well decide to become accustomed to this interesting
faculty, which will soon operate only when you have
cause to take an interest in what is behind you; or,
if it is really too disturbing, you may decide firmly to
see only as you do in your physical body. Some
people decide to image their "Key Figure" in a kind
of robe or cloak with a hood drawn up over the back
of the head.

While on the subject of extra faculties, it's worth
noting, for those who have some physical disability
such as short sight, deafness or the loss of a limb,
*that no such disability need be reproduced in the
astral vehicle.* IF YOU HAVE ANY DISABILITY
YOU CAN IN FACT DO YOURSELF A GREAT
DEAL OF GOOD, BY TAKING CARE *NOT* TO
IMAGINE IT INTO YOUR ASTRAL VEHICLE.

The hospitals have discovered by experience the
importance of training people who have lost a limb,
to maintain an imaginative awareness of the
continued reality of that limb. For such matters as
short sight however, much less research has been
done. *You can do your own research, to your
personal benefit.* It may take rather more courage and
determination than you initially expect. A person
who has for any number of years been accustomed
to some degree of lack, either in sight or in hearing,
for example, tends to stop looking or listening, as
the case may be, so as to avoid the emotional hurt of
failure. In other words, the lower self has begun to
"censor out" attempts in the direction of the deficient
sense, in order to avoid either disappointment or
humiliation (or even guilt feelings, if a child has been
punished for inattention when the real cause is
disability); the result often being that the physical
condition progressively becomes worse *to all
appearances,* as the person makes less and less effort

to utilize the ability he or she has.

It will surely be seen at once, without any need to labor the point, what new incentive, stimulation and encouragement such a person can gain by taking care to develop the "difficult" sense to maximum capacity *in the astral vehicle.*

Having through practice gained proficiency, then, in controlling the astral vehicle during short and familiar journeys, you can—and will—travel further afield. *Keep at first to the earthly level,* which is wide enough in all conscience to occupy and interest anyone for a considerable time.

One thing you may need to learn, is to regulate the amount of astral substance you have with you on your travels.

Most frequently, beginners tend to exteriorize a quite unnecessarily large amount of astral substance for the formulation of their vehicle. The same applies, sometimes, to the Formula of the Watcher, and you may in either case receive a rather embarrassing intimation of this, *when people who are not remarkably psychic become aware of activities of yours that you hadn't intended to make known.* Of course, a few people may be more psychic than you thought; but if this seems to apply to too many of your friends, you may well be employing too much astral substance; while if you wish to escape the notice of those who are "psychically aware," your best plan is to use less astral substance anyway.

On the other hand, if while in your astral vehicle YOU WISH TO GIVE "HEALING" (energy or astral substance) TO ANYONE, then you may want to have available a greater supply of astral material than you have equipped yourself with. *Bring it along the cord from your physical body*; this is done by the imaginative effort of "willing" it to you along the cord, plus a sensation rather like drawing the breath in. Not unnaturally, human language is rather deficient in appropriate words to describe any purely astral experience, so these comparisons can only be a general guide to sensations and techniques you will readily learn by experience.

As to the method of transferring energy to anyone, the surest way of doing this is just as you would do it while in your physical body: that is, to direct it through the hands of your astral vehicle just as you would direct it through your physical hands. One very probable difference, however, is that *when you do this in a state of astral projection, the energy or substance you are sending will be visible to you with no effort at visualization.*

At some time in your astral explorations, you are likely to wish to see something of the "native inhabitants" of the astral world, the Elementals. The great range and variety of these reflects the wonderful scope of the astral world itself, which comprises many levels and many types of beings. The unpleasant kinds of entity mentioned in Question 4 of Chapter 2, are *scarcely ever* likely to be encountered away from human proximity, of the present or of the past. (This consideration really leads to one of our non-physical "pollution problems" which would go beyond the subject of this book, but we shall be giving some thought to it.) So if you want to meet with the Elementals, travel astrally into a country region. An experienced astral traveller could go to a chosen spot physically, and *then* go forth, leaving his physical body meanwhile in a hotel bed, but it's advisable until you have quite a lot of practice, to leave your body only in your projection area at home.

Then, when you are in a suitable unspoiled locality, and in your astral vehicle, *send back some of your astral substance "along the cord"* so as to take yourself to the less material levels. Don't overdo this. Remember, the different "levels" in the astral world are NOT like the different levels you can reach in an elevator, where it's important not to stop between floors. WHEREVER you stop in the Astral World, you will find you are SOMEWHERE. In making your first explorations away from the earth level, however, there are a few points to be aware of.

First, the further you travel away from earth level, the more astral material you send back, the more will your mode of movement differ from physical modes of movement. We notice something very similar to this, of course, in physical life when climbing a high mountain; but on an earthly mountain we can only jettison some of our gear, we can't reduce the bulk of our earthly bodies to meet the new conditions.

Some astral travelers, as a fact, are never conscious of sending astral substance back along the cord; there are many who never even think about the cord. If they want to reach a high or less physical level, they just "will" themselves there, and the act of making the transfer looks after the surplus astral substance. Either way, however, you will find that a more gliding movement has to be adopted, to move at the higher levels.

There are, in practice, limits to the rising in the astral world that you can do; and while these limits will to some extend depend on the amount of experience you have, they do also depend on the sort of person you are. To reach the higher levels does take some form of dedication, and what in old-fashioned language is termed "detachment from earthly things." This is not, to be candid, a clear-cut way of estimating "moral" values, and it is very much one of those matters in which "what is right for one is wrong for another;" everyone has to make an individual decision.

BUT THE WHOLE GLORIOUS ASTRAL
WORLD IS THERE, WITH ITS INHABITANTS,
FROM THOSE BEINGS—SOME QUAINT AND
FANTASTIC, SOME INTENSELY LOVELY—THAT
WE CALL THE NATURE SPIRITS, UP TO THOSE
HIGH AND WONDERFUL ENTITIES OF LIVING
LIGHT THAT WE NAME ANGELS. THEY ARE
ALL PRESENT AT THEIR OWN LEVELS, AND
SOME CAN BE CONVERSED WITH: SOME CAN
ONLY BE MARVELLED AT.

It may well be a surprise to you that "angels" are
referred to as "astral" beings. This should give you a
true idea of the breadth, beauty and grandeur of the
astral world and the thrill and adventure of exploring
it. Some occultists are fond of referring to certain
phenomena as "only" astral, in a scathing tone.
EITHER THEY DON'T KNOW WHAT THEY ARE
TALKING ABOUT, OR THEY ARE PRETENDING
TO A HIGH SPIRITUAL DEVELOPMENT WHICH
THEY DON'T POSSESS. NO TRUE SAINT,
MYSTIC OR ADEPT WOULD EXPRESS ANY-
THING BUT LOVE, WONDER AND REVERENCE
FOR THE WONDERFUL ASTRAL WORLD. This is
true even of the material world; how much more,
then, it is true of the astral.
The Qabalah, that venerable and precise guide to
all the Worlds which has been revised and added to
by sages, scholars and seers of different races and

Adventures in the Astral Worlds.

centuries, is clear on these points. The astral world, in the language of the Qabalah, is the World of Yetzirah; and the Angels, the Intelligences, and the Elementals, are of Yetzirah.

But if some regions of the Astral World are beyond my reach, what happens?—what prevents me from getting there?

It is a double process. As you become more used to astral exploration, you can to some extent press onward to the less earthly regions by divesting yourself of more and more astral substance, like that climber toiling up the mountain. And, eventually, it *is* toil. Eventually you come to a halt. You can, if you like, rest at that point for a while, and then return. That is sensible. If you try to go on by sending back still more astral substance, *you may easily find you haven't left yourself enough for the kind of astral body which AT YOUR STAGE OF PERSONAL DEVELOPMENT you need.* The greater your degree of "personal progress" or "mystical evolution," the less astral substance you need for an adequate vehicle; but what this means in terms of actual power of ascent, you can only discover experimentally.

And supposing I DO inadvertently send back too much astral substance and haven't as much as I need for an adequate vehicle?—what happens then?

Then, you return instantly to your physical body, and most likely with the unpleasant kind of "snap back" we have mentioned earlier. This relates also to the fact that if you didn't eject sufficient astral substance initially, you couldn't move in your vehicle and probably would fail to transfer into it at all. Your own experimentation in these matters is the only sure guide FOR YOU.

You now know some important facts about the AMOUNT of astral substance that it is desirable for you to use.

More is excellent for anything involving the earth level: if you want to communicate with a person who is in his or her physical body, if you want to give energy or astral substance to anyone who needs it, if you want to travel in earthly or near-earthly localities. Or if as a *very* experienced astral traveler you desire to visit for some good purpose, and well protected, those polluted and corrupt regions of the Lower Astral which correspond to the "hells" described in various religions—the realms of nightmare, and the abodes of horror known to alcoholics and to the addicts of some narcotics. The psychologists say these are "purely subjective." Perhaps they were, at one time; but *to the creative human psyche, nothing remains purely subjective for long.* Hence, our reference to the Lower Astral as "polluted and corrupt." The question sometimes heard: "How could a just

God create . . . ?" is as inane as it would be to ask
"How could a just God create unstable and noxious
plastics?" We human beings have to learn to shoulder
our own responsibilities. In order to do that, naturally,
we must be able to recognize them; and here, again,
looking behind the scenes in the astral world will
teach us much.

Less astral substance renders us less perceptible
to people in their physical bodies, even to the moder-
ately psychic ones. It enables us to travel further and
faster, it enables us to rise higher. As against these
advantages, it reduces our power of action *until we
learn to act by methods which are more mental and
spiritual*, and it increases our danger of "snap-back"
to the physical body.

Meanwhile, don't worry. You are not at all likely
to find your way into the "hells" by mistake—it
needs a real effort to get down there. Visit a person
or a place that is of concern to you—or look at your
own physical body, with a question in mind about
your own concerns—then go to a higher level, still
relating to the same scene, and you will find valuable
material to reflect upon, both at the time and later
when you can bring the whole of your brain-apparatus

to bear on it. Besides problem-solving, there is a tremendous amount of adventure and delight awaiting you.

Before going on to the matter of astral adventure FOR TWO, there is another subject that needs to be touched upon. There are undoubtedly certain benevolent beings who take an intense interest in at least some of the events that take place at lower levels than their own, and who wish sometimes to call upon the services of a capable human being who is not yet so highly evolved as to be unable to reach those levels. You may, in fact, be on occasion aroused from sleep (or even from a daytime spell of reverie) with the clear knowledge that you are being called out into the astral world and conducted to some necessary task in which you can help. Performing such a task is always rewarding in terms of experience and personal maturity gained; it usually also requires a real effort and expenditure of energy, and it can in some instances be emotionally harrowing. *Your astral vehicle is made of the stuff of your emotional and instinctual self,* and so it is to be expected that your view of these happenings would be more emotional and less intellectual than your normal viewpoint; but, if the Helpers didn't think you could "take it," they would not have chosen you. It is of no use, either, to question why, amidst all the trouble and suffering in the world, some matters are chosen for intervention and not others. The Helpers are probably not omniscient; perhaps they have special interests in special cases; perhaps there are not enough of them, quite likely there are not enough of us humans who can be effectively called upon for astral work; probably also there are karmic reasons which are not made known to us, destinies for particular individuals to fulfill, links between the Helpers and those helped, links between ourselves and the one or the other. Be these things as they may, there are some suicides that have to be prevented, some deaths that have to be eased, some self-punished souls that have to be aroused from a remorse no longer productive, to reassert the special talents they misused in a lifetime now past. *When you are called upon, you will be conducted, you will understand what to do, you will be given whatever strength and protection you need, and you will be brought back afterwards.*

And, you will realize how lovable are all sorts of people you would not have thought you could love. Read again Walt Whitman's great poem, *The Sleepers*, with new insight.

Astral Travel for Two

It seems natural that two people who share the same interests and are generally very close to one another, should be able to explore and enjoy the astral world in each other's company. This is in reality the case, so long as care is taken over a few matters.

There are some simple guidelines that apply whatever may be the relationship of the two: be they lovers, close friends, brothers, sisters or parent and child. If one is considerably experienced in astral travel and the other a beginner, there is little difficulty: the experienced one can leave the body—whether in the physical company of the other or not is usually unimportant—and can give the novice a great deal of telepathic encouragement in forming and in projecting into his or her own astral vehicle. As soon as the learner is "airborne," of course, the teacher's astral form will be clearly visible to the newcomer, just as the astral substance you give to another is clearly visible to you while you are in your astral vehicle.

It is sometimes said that when a learner receives help from a teacher in astral projection, the learner fails to become proficient in the sense of being afterwards able to carry out the procedure unaided. This, so far as it is true, may not matter to some who mean only to travel together; but experience seems to show that the danger only exists when the teacher assists in the actual formation of the learner's astral vehicle. As is stated a little earlier in this chapter, attempted projection into an inadequate astral vehicle makes journeying impossible and, indeed, makes successful projection itself improbable. THE LEARNER SHOULD, THEREFORE, RIGHT FROM THE BEGINNING, eject his or her astral substance and from this—and only from this—should form his or her own astral vehicle. Besides this, the learner should in any case have worked individually through the regimen and the Formulae given in this book. NO OTHER PERSON'S EXPERIENCE CAN TAKE THE PLACE OF THIS INDIVIDUAL TRAINING; IT HAS TO BE PART OF THE LEARNER'S OWN LIFE-EXPERIENCE.

There are rather more difficulties when both the intended partners in astral travel are beginners together. Practice in company is a doubtful benefit. The two can give each other a great deal of help in other ways—for instance, they can take turns in sending a Watcher to each other, and the one who is acting as "host" can keep notes of the events of the day so that the other's impressions can be afterwards verified; or, if a specific time for the presence of the Watcher is not stated, the "host" can let the other partner know afterwards if the presence of the Watcher is by any means detected! But with regard to the Simulacrum, DETAILS OF WHAT ANY PERSON HAS TO SAY TO HIS OR HER LOWER SELF SHOULD NEVER BE DISCUSSED WITH AN INTIMATE FRIEND OR RELATIVE. Read books on psychology or on self-hypnosis—you can learn from them even though your technique is different—talk to people with experience in psychotherapy if you can glean ideas without danger to your own program; but DON'T discuss your inner weaknesses with anyone with whom you are emotionally linked. In such a context as this, the man was right who said "I am the weaker for every ally who rallies to my banner."

Again, with regard to Formula Four, certainly notes can very well be compared on progress, *but great care is needed if two novices make their first attempt at projection of consciousness together.* Interest in each other's achievement, even if silence is maintained, is extremely likely to keep drawing the attention of each one back to the physical presence of the other. At the same time, if they are apart but practicing at the same hour, the first one to succeed is likely to be particularly tempted to pay a premature astral visit to the other; premature, because as we have said, THE FIRST SUCCESS IS NOT THE RIGHT OCCASION FOR VENTURING OUT OF THE PROJECTION AREA, and also, because such a visit may upset the partner's chances of success on that occasion. Restraint is best.

Each of the intending partners should, therefore, try for proficiency independently; but *as soon as one of them achieves this to the extent of being able to travel*, then a visit is natural, and can be very helpful to the other partner, as has been indicated.

WHEN BOTH ARE PROFICIENT, THEN EITHER ONE CAN "CALL FOR" THE OTHER, OR AN AGREEMENT CAN BE MADE TO MEET, AS-TRALLY, AT A GIVEN MATERIAL LANDMARK. Such arrangements are known to work very well.

Joint travel of this kind is not only very enjoyable, it affords an extra verification of the reality of the various experiences, when the two partners afterwards compare notes. This, especially, calls for the keeping of a diary by each person. If there is some disagree-ment between the two accounts, this is only to be expected; human beings are like that, even when they have their "card index" brains with them! Two such accounts, with their discrepancies of one sort and another, in fact give an additional dimension of reality to the occurrence, just as the slightly different viewpoint between a pair of stereoscopic photographs is what gives depth to the scene. Verbatim exactness would suggest telepathy rather than a shared ex-perience.

A fascinating variant from the more serious and earnest types of astral travel can be indulged in if both partners happen to have a taste for masquerade. To give examples here would be difficult, because in this matter, what is sheer delight to one pair might be the worst of taste to another; but evidently, for one's own enjoyment and for that of a chosen partner, all kinds of variations in the form of the astral vehicle are possible. They might be varied from one occasion to another according to the site to be visited; a game which caused a great deal of mischievous amusement to one couple, who, after visiting a historic scene in suitable astral attire, solely for their own pleasure and with "no intent to deceive," heard a subsequent rumor that the place was "haunted" by two "ghosts" who could only have been themselves.

Any experienced psychic investigator would know, we must add, the astral forms of two incarnate human beings from other kinds of apparitions, whether "spirits" or not.

Astral Sex — Supreme Rapture!

Strangely enough, quite a lot of people, when they speak of "astral sex," mean the type of sexual activity that is possible when one of the partners *only* is out in an astral vehicle, the other being in his or her physical body. As this is what people so often ask about, it seems best to deal with it at the outset here, before going on to describe the real thing.

The true flames of passion—Astral Fire.

If one of the partners is remaining in the physical body, farewell to the equality of the sexes!—for the advantage here is all on the side of Woman. SHE can go forth, in a "heavy" (i.e., near-physical) astral vehicle which can be as beauteous and seductive as she pleases; SHE can seek out her chosen mate, no matter what earthly barrier divides them, and can spend tireless hours of bliss in his company; indeed, by taking from him more astral substance, which he will readily yield to her, she can, for that time, bring her astral vehicle even nearer to materialization. Many men, parted from wife or lover, have experienced this kind of visitation, and, if they did not know what was happening, have marveled at the intense vividness of their "dreams."

Man, however, is at a distinct disadvantage if he seeks to pay a similarly amorous visit. He may, indeed, form for himself a suitable astral vehicle—and many men, especially in time of war, have done this spontaneously even if they have never travelled astrally before. He can transfer his consciousness into it and can journey into the physical proximity of his beloved. Up to a certain point, too, he can embrace her and can delight in her bodily presence.

What he cannot achieve in these circumstances is orgasm. THE GREAT AMOUNT OF ASTRAL SUBSTANCE THAT HE WOULD NEED FOR ORGASM WITH A PHYSICALLY PRESENT PARTNER IS MORE THAN HE CAN HAVE IN HIS ENTIRE ASTRAL VEHICLE, and the result of making the attempt is—*instantly*—a snap-back to his own physical body. There is no way around this: if he attempted to draw astral substance along the cord, the great amount called upon would cause a reverse action, so that this in itself would, at once, snap him back.

Plenty of women (and not by any means all of them the right type of victim for the classic "old maid's delusion") have had the experience of sexual encounter with astral entities; but in no case, *if the woman was definitely in her physical body at the time*, can her partner have been an astrally embodied, incarnate human male. AT LEAST—it can't have been if orgasm took place *on his part*, which is another condition she might not be clear about if her own experience was intense.

If she was at that time out of her physical body, then the complete encounter becomes quite feasible—and, of course, becomes quite a different matter. She may deny that it can have been an "astral experience," just because few people have any idea of the intense rapture of out-of-the-body sexual experience. Many a lonely wife whose absent husband pays her an astral visit, must have gone forth unknowingly from her own body to meet him.

When both partners are proficient in astral experience generally, and intend sexual pleasure in the astral world, forming their astral vehicles accordingly, the result is beyond earthly expectation. Not the physical body which can be so slow in response, not the intellect which can raise its own barriers, but the emotional and instinctual nature is almost alone concerned in the making of the astral vehicle; the rational mind will interpose only to add some extra refinement of bliss. Everyone knows how the whole natural world is enhanced with color and freshness and bloom in the mating season; even so will a new glowing brilliance, charm and vibrant sensitivity be added by the instinctual nature itself to enhance these astral shapes.

So both partners go forth to their astral meeting in these radiant forms. As they approach one another, they will be able to see joy and desire reflected each in the other, not only in their astral vehicles themselves but in the changeful and lovely aura of vivid colors surrounding each; colors which, as the lovers unite in an embrace that is an entire ecstasy, flash and whirl and coruscate in rainbow hues, climaxing into golden flame.

This, furthermore, is only the first step. The lovers can remain at that point, making their astral sex as close as possible to its earthly counterpart; or they can discover more. If they watch the elemental beings at play, they will assuredly learn more, for, although there is not "sex" among those beings, there is delight unbounded; and the human onlookers can come also to realize that every part of the astral shape is capable of giving and of receiving subtle energies, interchanges of delight. *Why not?—for it is all truly of one same substance,* however much the newcomers, fashioning forms and seeking pleasures for themselves in their accustomed kind, may have tried to limit its nature within the limitations of flesh.

The earthly body has "erogenous zones" and "non-erogenous zones;" while the "union," "coitus" or "intercourse" of any two individuals, no matter how passionate they may be, is really limited to a small proportion of the physical frame and is almost a misnomer. It indicates what the lovers desire to achieve, not what really is the case. Two such lovers, in their first explorations of the possibilities of astral union, may at first believe it necessary to observe some such limitations in their astral forms. Or, indeed, they may at once transcend those limitations, and may discover at once the true nature of astral union: not an interpenetration but a total merging, each into each, so that while that rapture lasts they do, indeed, burn as a single flame.

Love-play, however, of which the elemental world is full, is something else, a truly playful mode of giving and of taking, in passing, small charges of energy that are something between a caress and an electric shock but wholly pleasurable. Humans, in the astral world, can do the same. It is also possible, literally, to "throw a kiss" to a person, simply by forming (at the fingertips) a small astral ball, willing energy into it and tossing it; the recipient experiences a kind of "electrical kiss"—and can toss it back, recharged! It's true, as some observers have noted, that the Nature-spirits play at "innocent childish games"—but don't underestimate them!

(While much can be learned from the Elementals, it is always a good thing for everyone's sake if you avoid getting in too deeply with them. Some of them love imitating humans, and this does them no good, while you on your side could become completely confused as to the borderline between their real nature and the imitation of humanity. We should just take pleasure in their enjoyment of their own kind of life and happiness.)

For human couples, however, the enhancement of life to be gained from a sexual approach to astral projection is immense. The sharing of every kind of exploration in the astral realms makes, in itself, for an inner companionship which few can enjoy within the boundaries of physical existence alone—the sharing of limitless travels, adventures and deep insights. With regard to their sex-life, the dimensions both of variety and of understanding will bring a great enrichment also into their physical relationship.

To begin with, the extreme plasticity and response of the astral form to every emotional stimulus, will, from the beginning, clear away all those doubts and shadowy misunderstandings which so often creep into the physical relationship as a result of some inability or inhibition, on the part of one of the partners, which prevents the full expression of all the love and passion that may be felt.

Again, the possibilities of masquerade that have been mentioned as heightening, for some couples, the pleasure of astral experience generally, take on a new significance when applied to experiences of astral sex. Just as at carnival time, from the Middle Ages onward, disguise and changed aspect could be employed to reveal, rather than to hide, aspects of the personalities of the masqueraders, and people found new and unexpected loves or—frequently—an astonishing new and exciting aspect in an old love, so it is with the changeable astral form. Shapes of all kinds are possible, if the will and the imagination of the lovers can extend to them; and the memory of such experiences and such revelations of the inner resources of the couple can be brought back, to vitalize earthly forms of union in less adaptable conditions. This, in itself, will help to clear away any tensions in the physical relationship which might have been due to hidden frustrations and inhibitions.

This is particularly true of those frustrations and inhibitions which exist when a man feels his sexual role denies all expression to the feminine or receptive side of his nature; or a woman feels her role denies any expression to her own positive and dominant impulses. All these things can be acted out in the astral world, either with an exchange of roles, or, if that is desired, even an exchange of shapes.

With all these possibilities of pleasure, there is another very great benefit that is likely to come gradually, and in greatest measure, to those couples who in their astral union progress from any imitation of earthly intercourse to the "merging" which astral form makes possible. That, and the delicate kinds of love-play that are so blissfully and yet easily possible in astral life, will effect a great release from ingrained and unhappy habits of Western thought.

It cannot be denied, that instead of sex being as it should be (everyone's doorway of release from anxiety, from over-seriousness, from the pressures of duty and of convention), even between the most dedicated of lovers, it frequently is only the way into a network of other anxieties, worries, false ideas of obligation and of conventions to be fulfilled. One of the worst of these pressures is the idea of the amount of sheer exertion which has to be put into the whole thing. Especially, of course, there is the idea of the obligation of orgasm. This anxiety is such that, if, for example, the partners feel on some particular occasion that they are too tired to guarantee reaching that conclusion, they will avoid each other's embrace altogether.

Such an attitude is based on tragic nonsense, and here the remembered experiences of astral sex will help immeasurably. The partners will not need incessant physical reassurance as to each other's emotional response, nor will they believe that to be "worthwhile" an embrace must always go to extremes of demonstration. This emancipation from various stresses and tensions will naturally make it easier for them to succeed in finding great enjoyment where previously they only feared to fail.

In all these aspects of greater mutual confidence, understanding and lighthearted fun, besides deep companionship, the partners will have been brought by astral sex into something nearer to the spiritual atmosphere of the Eastern cults of TANTRA and of TAO than is usual in a Western relationship. It is also a fact that the recommendations made in this book with regard to diet and to physical exercise, *with the repeated vitalization of the Centres of Activity in the use of Formula One*, will have brought their lifestyle near to those ancient ideals. (Learn more about them and discover further adventures!)

That does not say astral experience is at all "typically oriental." It is to say that it is a way of return from artificial and over-rationalized modern standards, into something universally and ideally human.

The present chapter by no means exhausts the possibilities of activity in the astral world; there is, for the more advanced practitioner especially, much that could be added. This book, however, is for the purpose of *helping you to make a beginning* in out-of-the-body experience, and this it should do IF YOU

FOLLOW IT THROUGH FULLY AND IN SE-
QUENCE, with care and patience. Some people do,
of course, take a lot longer than others to shed
feelings of unbelief and such-like barriers.

When you have attained proficiency in astral
travel itself and can move freely in your astral vehicle
both at the earth level and somewhat above it,
DON'T FORGET TO CONTINUE WITH THE
OTHER FORMULAE IN THIS BOOK, ESPECIALLY
FORMULA ONE! Keep up your health and diet
regimen too, and so continue to grow in experience
and happiness.

Check Point

7

NOW YOU CAN LEAVE YOUR BODY SUC-
CESSFULLY:

● *Begin with* SHORT ASTRAL JOURNEYS *at
"earth level."* Then travel further.
● *Discover ways in which your astral vehicle has*
GREATER SENSE-FACULTIES *than your earthly
body; especially* with regard to any bodily disabilities.
● *Discover how to* CONTROL YOUR ASTRAL
VEHICLE *and to regulate the amount of astral sub-
stance according to your various purposes.*

● *Get to know the* WORLD OF THE ELE-
MENTALS.

- *Learn to "look behind the scenes" by CHANG-ING LEVELS.*
- *Be ready to "HELP THE HELPERS" if called upon.*
- *TRAVEL WITH A COMPANION and compare notes—it's much more fun!*
- *Try ASTRAL MASQUERADE.*
- *ASTRAL SEX IS WONDERFUL!*
- *WIDEN YOUR UNDERSTANDING, both by REFLECTING on your adventures, and by READING.*

- *Work through this book, then keep up the various practices—ESPECIALLY FORMULA ONE!* BE READY FOR MORE EXPERIENCE—WE'VE ONLY SAID A LITTLE IN THIS BOOK ABOUT THE "HIDDEN WORLDS" YOU CAN REACH.

Adventure in the Astral Worlds

Personal Notes

Adventure in the Astral Worlds

APPENDIX

TWO ILLUSTRATIONS OF ASTRAL EXPERIENCE

Study Points

Appendix

1. A case history of astral attack.

2. A case history of sleep-projection during which conscious control is exerted. Points illustrated include:
   a. The presence of the rational mind in realizing the out-of-the-body situation.
   b. The emotional response to authority symbols that inhibits the role of the rational mind and during astral projection.
   c. The ability to reach a person without knowing the exact location.
   d. Penetration of physical barriers.
   e. The effect of psychic barriers.
   f. Overcoming the psychic barrier through the desire to be of help.

g. The awareness of the astral presence by the recipient of the healing.

h. The ability of the person in the astral to look "beneath-the-surface" of the problem.

i. The various differences in the ways of "thinking" observed.

AN EXAMPLE OF ASTRAL COMBAT

The following account is excerpted from a much longer account, forming part of an appendix to Volume IV of The Magical Philosophy, *of intermittent experiences spread over a considerable period of time with a malevolent astral entity. Most of the experiences are of an unpleasant kind of "haunting" by this entity, but the crisis of the affair is the astral combat here described. It is also referred to, briefly, under Question 4 in Chapter 2 of this book.*

Having become accustomed to sleeping with the lamp alight, I found no difficulty about this. Presently, however, I dreamed that I awakened; or to put it in a different way, I did awaken, but on to the far

side of consciousness instead of back to the waking
state. In this condition, and as if obeying an instruction, my consciousness but not my body went out
through the closed door and waited. I felt as if it
were protected, though I cannot say with what; and
when something came rushing from afar and leapt
upon me, aiming for my neck, the shock which I
felt was the sheer horror of contact rather than fear
of the event. Yet I felt I was battling for my life,
albeit by choice.

It is difficult to describe this pseudo-physical
grappling. The movements of it were instinctive,
but not, I think, actually intended by either party for
the infliction of bodily wounds, had that been
possible. The purpose was partly to instill fear, but
chiefly, on either side, to make unceasingly felt the
strength of one's own resolution and at the same
time to test continually the resolution of the adversary. It was, in essence, a battle of wills.

Two other notions presented themselves to me
as facts. One was that as we struggled we were
progressively rising into thinner, purer atmosphere;
the other was that we were not alone. Even apart
from the darkness in which we still seemed to be
enveloped, I could not have spared an instant's
attention for anything but the contest; yet to some
area of my mind which was free from it, it seemed
that there were watchers, perhaps in the function
of seconds in a duel. I do not know whether they
would have intervened, or upon what conditions; for

all I know, they may indeed have intervened, but my one certainty is that there was a plurality of them, and they were present. As to my adversary, I can only state that it was all menace, with no possibility of compromise. I fought it in horror and loathing but I would not let it depart undefeated. And then suddenly, at what seemed my last resource of endurance, the thing fell away and was gone. I awoke trembling and gasping, but free.

The comparison with Robert A. Monroe's account, also referred to under Question 4 in Chapter 2, is of great interest because of the similar human reaction to what seems to have been a very similar type of lower astral assailant. Both Robert Monroe and the anonymous woman narrator in the account just given mention resemblances of the assailant to a dog, although in intelligence and in mode of assault it was clearly something other than a dog, astral or otherwise. In its un-doglike aspects, too, Robert Monroe's assailant seems to have been of similar type to the other. We can add that there is no possibility of any connection between the two texts. The interested reader is referred to Robert A. Monroe's book, Journeys Out of the Body, *Chapter 10, particularly the passage beginning:* "The struggle was not like fending off an animal. It was a no-holds-barred affair, silent, terrifyingly fast, and with the other seeking out any weakness on my part. I did not fight back savagely at first, because I was bewildered. I merely tried to defend myself."

UNTRAINED ASTRAL TRAVEL

It has been mentioned (on page 36) that an experience of astral projection, begun involuntarily in sleep, can be taken over by the conscious mind of the sleeper and can be turned into a purposeful adventure.

An example of this type of action is transcribed below, with comments, from Volume IV of The Magical Philosophy. *The person who had this experience was a woman who at that time had no idea of any technique for deliberate transfer of consciousness out of the body. Readers interested in the Qabalistic and psychosophical theory of different forms of out-of-the-body experience are referred to* The Magical Philosophy *in general, and Volume IV in particular.*

Laura was an unmarried woman of higher than average I.Q., but with a strongly emotional nature who without any occult training had been an occasional "astral traveler" from childhood; she had in some instances been seen by percipients of only moderate sensitivity, who had the impression that she wore a trailing pale-coloured dress. She had also a slight history of physical sleepwalking in her late teens. . . . It does not appear that she had ever had any conscious technique for leaving her body, which according to her sister lay in an almost cataleptic and unwakeable sleep meanwhile; she had to wait for occasions when, for unknown reasons, she "found herself outside," as she put it, and then she simply decided where she would go and what she would do. Nothing in connection with these adventures had ever frightened her, nor had she ever experienced any difficulty in returning to her body afterwards. It must be added that she was thoroughly accustomed to life in a large town, and was in the usual style of commercial employment.

On the occasion in question, which was during her twenty-seventh year, she awakened one night to find herself apparently walking along the street near her home. Several circumstances convinced her that she was not dreaming: there was, to some extent, the mere fact that she had questioned the matter, although she did not consider this to be an infallible test; then the fact which had first caught her attention, that she heard no sound of her own footsteps as she moved forward. Besides this, she felt no slightest impact of air upon her skin; and again—a rather curious point—there was the fact that she felt it to be a certain definite time during the night, perhaps an hour after midnight, which would make it about two and a half hours since she had gone to bed. In dreams, she commented, it might seem like daytime or night-time, but it never seemed to be a certain time which could be related to the hour at which one had gone to bed. Apart from these matters, however, she felt, although she did not explore the situation in any detail, that she was quite her usual self. What, now (she had wondered), should she take this opportunity to do? She called to mind a man with whom she worked; he suffered from some form of heart trouble, but, although she liked and respected him, she knew little about him, for he was rather unusually quiet and reserved. She knew he lived in the next town, perhaps ten miles away. She resolved to go and see whether she could do anything to help his state of health. The fact that she did not know his address did not trouble her; she knew, in any case, the way to the general area, and resolved that when she arrived there, she would "think of where he was and just go there," as she put it.

Up to this point—that is, up to her actual setting out on the astral journey—her description of her mental processes seems normal, in the general sense of the word; only through knowing her usual style and manner does one perceive that it is all rather too naive to be truly natural—as if, even to bring the episode back to recollection some years afterward, she had had to put into abeyance a considerable part of her habitual vitality and discursiveness. No comment on this was however made at the time; and without interruption she continued her account.

About half a mile from her home, she had to cross a main road. It was a wide arterial road and at most hours of day or night, there would be some traffic upon it, frequently a considerable amount; but at that moment it was deserted. She considered crossing its bare expanse, but although she hesitated for some time, the traffic signals remained green. She did not know what to do. Would she be visible to the driver of a vehicle? Would a vehicle be visible to her? She no longer felt quite sure. What would happen if a vehicle, perhaps invisible to her, were to strike her in her present state? She stood by the traffic lights, trying to work this out from basic principles and slowly realizing that her "brain was not working"; then, despairing of an answer and feeling that she was wasting valuable time, she summoned up her courage and went forward across the road.

Her narrative contains nothing further to our purpose until we find her standing outside a tall detached house in which, she realized, her friend lived. She hesitated between trying to ascend to an open window, or going to the front door; then she decided on the side door, because "people often leave their side doors unlocked." She found the door and was about to turn the handle when suddenly she remembered that whether it might be locked or unlocked, her hands would have no physical strength. Again she stood in a dejected state of indecision for some time until, slowly, the answer came to her: since she was "out without her body," the door could present no barrier to her; she had but to go boldly onward, willing herself to be inside the house, and inside she would be. After a moment, she realized that she had passed the threshold and was now in the kitchen. Several people, she felt, were in the house; she accordingly fixed her mind on the personality of her friend, succeeded in singling out the particular feeling of his presence, and followed it as it became stronger, into the next room, up the stairs, and to another closed door. Once more, taught by experience, she thought to advance without hindrance; but this time, despite her struggles, she could not at once succeed. She deliberately considered in her mind the intended work of healing which was her purpose there; then she redoubled her efforts to get in. At last she succeeded, but, as she puts it, "it was like going through a fine-mesh sieve." She crossed the room (observing a bedside lamp which she afterwards described accurately) to look at the person lying in the bed. Compelling herself to see beneath the surface, she arrived at a conclusion as to the nature of the infirmity and then carried out her work of healing. Of her return home, she states that she remembered only the moment when she was standing at her own bedside, looking down at her unconscious body. Then, as she leaned over it, to quote her own words once more, "One moment I was looking downwards, and then there was a sort of click and I found I was staring up at the ceiling from the bed where I lay." The next morning at work, her friend thanked her for *what she had done*, and told her it was the first morning for some months that he had been able to start the day without digitalin; there was later evidence too of the reality of the improvement in his condition.

Laura's account, then, gives us as direct insight as possible into the levels of experience where the mind must operate without the physical brain. With regard to the limited descriptive ability previously remarked, Laura was asked when her story was completed, why she had felt it necessary to speak in this way. She replied that she had spoken as she had felt at the time of her occurrence, because she wanted to be certain of adding nothing. Her thinking had been very simple during that experience, because she had felt rather as if she had been partially stunned: "If I could have been hit on the

head without feeling any pain or discomfort from it,
I think I should have felt as I did while I was out of
my body. It was like a sort of keeping on coming
back into reality."

In other words, Laura had felt her sense of
continuity to be mildly impaired, as in slight con-
cussion. This is of some interest as cases are recorded
of other persons, differing from Laura in that they
were not known to be recurrent astral travelers, but
citing their sole experience of detached consciousness
as being the consequence of a fall, of delirium (e.g.
in malaria), or of comparable circumstances. Inquiry
failed to show any comparable history in Laura's
case, however; she and both her parents enjoyed
robust health, and none of her experiences of extra-
corporeal awareness had been associated with any
illness, accident, or drug. In all cases, she had simple
gone to bed as usual, without even a premonition of
what was going to occur. It can therefore be confidently put forward that the "concussed" state of
mind which she describes was an effect, and not a
cause, of the separation of her consciousness from
her body.

We perceive her mind, then, seeking but not
finding access to its familiar brain-index; as a matter
of psychological interest, we notice that being deprived
of that material, the inculcated veto upon crossing a
road in defiance of the traffic signals asserts a considerably greater authority than it would over her
normal mode of thought. Ordinarily, her practical

sense would certainly not have hesitated before crossing a manifestly empty road regardless of the signals; but in her projected state, the authority of the traffic lights had to be rationalized, so that she even forgot that she was now less vulnerable to physical harm than in her physical body. Again, we have her hesitation as to how to enter the house. It is evident, apart from any other aspect of the matter, that excepting the slight and barely perceived amnesic sensations, Laura's consciousness in her astral body does not strike her as being very different from the everyday situation in her physical body.

Something very different takes place when she attempts to enter her friend's room. It is a well-known fact that the development of the higher faculties gives a resistant quality to the aura which enables it to repulse alien astral visitors; rarely indeed, however, can an account of the matter be secured from the viewpoint of the repulsed visitor. It is noteworthy that the boundary of the psychic barrier is identified in this particular instance—probably accurately—with the obstacle of the material door. But Laura's reaction to the difficulty is most interesting. Her purpose is to heal: it is tacitly made plain by her declaration that she has not come to injure or seduce by her intrusion. Quite probably, even apart from the effect of her declaration upon the developed intuitive powers of the man she was approaching, this deliberate recollection of her motives was necessary to release her own powers. We have seen how she hesitated to cross an empty road in defiance of the traffic regulations; the ordinary convention against entering the bedroom of a man whom she respected may well have made part of her difficulty in crossing the threshold. At all events, we are told that having declared her purpose, she was, without a further struggle, admitted.

(This is most likely, also, an instance where the "struggle" involved an unconscious sending-back of astral substance until it was needed for the actual healing, hence the "fine-mesh sieve" effect.)

GLOSSARY

Astral Bleeding *Involuntary loss of astral substance, usually from the solar plexus region.*

Astral Vehicle *"Body" formed of astral substance through which the consciousness can function separately from the physical body.*

Centres of Activity *Energy-centres of the astral body, corresponding to neural or glandular centres in the physical body.*

Circulation of the Light *Essential closing action of Formula One, when energy is re-circulated through the whole organism.*

Dream Diary *Special record of dreams kept for purposes of analysis or to examine the*

responses of the psyche to an inner program.

Higher Self *That part of the psyche which is more elevated than the rational mind: the Higher Unconscious, the Spirit.*

Lower Self *The soul and the physical body together: the rational, emotional, instinctual, lower unconscious and material levels of human nature.*

Nephesh *Qabalistic term for the emotional and instinctual levels collectively of the psyche: the "non-rational soul."*

Neshamah *Qabalistic term for the Higher Self.*

Noemasome *The Mental*

Body: sometimes called the Mental Sheath because its substance is so much finer than that of the Astral Body.

Out-of-the-Body Experience
A term generally synonymous with "Astral Projection" but sometimes preferable: it simply describes the effect without making any assumption as to the cause.

Posture   Any definite bodily position: compare the Yogic term "asana."

Psyche   The non-material part of a psycho-physical being.

Qabalah   A venerable Wisdom-tradition which has been formulated mainly in Mediterranean regions: Hebrew and Greek are its principal languages.

Rhythmic Breath   A method of steady breathing controlled according to a pre-determined rhythm.

Ruach   Qabalistic term for the rational consciousness: that part of the human psyche which should direct the Nephesh (q.v.) and should be receptive to the Neshamah (q.v.)

Simulacrum   A phantasmal replica: here, a replica of the operator, formed of exteriorized astral substance.

Snap-back   Sudden involuntary return of consciousness with the astral vehicle into the physical body, often with a disagreeable sense of shock.

Soul   Usual popular term for the psyche or for some part thereof.

Spirit   The highest part of the psyche, usually defined in mystical theology as "the fine point of the soul."

Watcher   A body of astral substance, not employed as a vehicle for the conscious mind but sent forth to gather *impressions on the material level.*

Worlds *The Four Worlds comprise the four levels of being envisaged by the Qabalah: the Divine/Spiritual, the Mental, the Astral World, the Material Universe. All are represented in human nature.*

STAY IN TOUCH

On the following pages you will find listed, with their current prices, some of the books now available on related subjects. Your book dealer stocks most of these and will stock new titles in the Llewellyn series as they become available. We urge your patronage.

TO GET A FREE CATALOG

To obtain our full catalog, you are invited to write (see address below) for our catalog, *Llewellyn's New Worlds of Mind and Spirit*. A sample copy is free, or you may subscribe for just $10 in the United States and Canada ($20 overseas, first class mail). Many bookstores also have *New Worlds* available to their customers. Ask for it.

TO ORDER BOOKS AND TAPES

If your book store does not carry the titles described on the following pages, you may order them directly from Llewellyn by sending the full price in U.S. funds, plus postage and handling (see below).

Credit Card Orders: VISA, MasterCard, American Express are accepted. Call toll-free within the USA and Canada at 1-800-THE-MOON.

Special Group Discount: Because there is a great deal of interest in group discussion and study of the subject matter of this book, we offer a 20% quantity discount to group leaders or agents. Our Special Quantity Price for a minimum order of five copies of *The Llewellyn Practical Guide to Astral Projection* is $39.80 cash-with-order. Include postage and handling charges noted below.

Postage and Handling: Include $4 postage and handling for orders $15 and under; $5 for orders *over* $15. There are no postage and handling charges for orders over $100. Postage and handling rates are subject to change. We ship UPS whenever possible within the continental United States; delivery is guaranteed. Please provide your street address as UPS does not deliver to P.O. boxes. Orders shipped to Alaska, Hawaii, Canada, Mexico and Puerto Rico will be sent via first class mail. Allow 4-6 weeks for delivery. **International orders:** Airmail – add retail price of each book and $5 for each non-book item (audiotapes, etc.); Surface mail – add $1 per item. Minnesota residents add 7% sales tax.

Mail orders to:
Llewellyn Worldwide
P.O. Box 6438, Dept. L181-4
St. Paul, MN 55164-0383, U.S.A.

For customer service, call 1-800-THE-MOON
In Minnesota, call (612) 291-1970.

THE LLEWELLYN PRACTICAL GUIDE TO
THE DEVELOPMENT OF PSYCHIC POWERS
Denning & Phillips

You may not realize it, but you already have the ability to use
ESP, Astral Vision and Clairvoyance, Divination, Dowsing,
Prophecy, and Communication with Spirits. Written by two of
the most knowledgeable experts in the world of psychic development, this book is a complete course—teaching you, step-
by-step, how to develop these powers that actually have been
yours since birth. Using the techniques, you will soon be able
to move objects at a distance, see into the future, know the
thoughts and feelings of another person, find lost objects and
locate water using your no-longer latent talents.

The text shows you how to make the equipment you can use,
the exercises you can do—many of them at any time, anywhere—and how to use your abilities to change your life and
the lives of those close to you. Many of the exercises are presented in forms that can be adapted as games for pleasure and
fun, as well as development.

0-87542-191-1, 272 pp., 5¼ x 8, illus., softcover $9.95

To order, call 1-800-THE-MOON
Prices subject to change without notice

GATEWAY TO THE ASTRAL WORLDS
Denning & Phillips

If you have had difficulty projecting in past attempts, this is the kit for you! It contains The Llewellyn Practical Guide to Astral Projection book, with the clearest and most explicit instructions on how to project out of the body; the "Llewellyn Deep Mind Tape for Astral Projection," featuring instructions, exercises, and special sounds that will help you prepare to project; a meditation card for inducing the altered state of consciousness; and a special instruction booklet.

No single item can help everyone to project, but this kit is so complete that your chances are considerably enhanced by its use. Astral projection is possible for everyone, as well as being a completely safe way to explore a fascinating array of new planes of reality and a previously unknown facet of your unconscious mind. For the ultimate vacation, take a trip on the astral plane!

0-87542-199-7, book, tape, booklet, meditation card $19.95

FLYING WITHOUT A BROOM
ASTRAL PROJECTION AND THE ASTRAL WORLD
D. J. Conway

Astral flight has been described through history as a vital part of spiritual development and a powerful aid to magickal workings. In this remarkable volume, respected author D.J. Conway shows how anyone can have the keys to a profound astral experience. This complete how-to includes historical lore, a groundwork of astral plane basics, and a simplified learning process to get you "off the ground." You'll learn simple exercises to strengthen your astral abilities as well as a variety of astral techniques—including bilocation and time travel. Through astral travel you will expand your spiritual growth, strengthen your spiritual efforts, and bring your daily life to a new level of integration and satisfaction.

1-56718-164-3, 224 pp., 6x9, softcover   **$13.00**

To order, call 1-800-THE-MOON
Prices subject to change without notice

THE LLEWELLYN PRACTICAL GUIDE TO CREATIVE VISUALIZATION
For the Fulfillment of Your Desires
Denning & Phillips

All things you will ever want must have their start in your mind. The average person uses very little of that full creative power. It's like the power locked in the atom—it's all there, but you have to learn to release it and apply it constructively.

This book changes that. Through an easy series of step-by-step, progressive exercises, your mind is applied to bring desire into realization! Wealth, power, success, happiness, psychic powers ... even what we call magickal power and spiritual attainment ... all can be yours. You can easily develop this completely natural power, and correctly apply it, for your immediate and practical benefit. Illustrated with unique, "puts-you-into-the-picture" visualization aids.

0-87542-183-0, 294 pp., 5¼ x 8, illus., softcover $8.95

THE LLEWELLYN ANNUALS

Llewellyn's MOON SIGN BOOK: Approximately 500 pages of valuable information on gardening, fishing, weather, stock market forecasts, personal horoscopes, good planting dates, and general instructions for finding the best date to do just about anything! Articles by prominent forecasters and writers in the fields of gardening, astrology, politics, economics and cycles. This special almanac, different from any other, has been published annually since 1906. It's fun, informative and has been a great help to millions in their daily planning. New larger 5¼ x 8 format. **State year $6.95**

Llewellyn's SUN SIGN BOOK: Your personal horoscope for the entire year! All 12 signs are included in one handy book. Also included are forecasts, special feature articles, and an action guide for each sign. Monthly horoscopes are written by Gloria Star, author of *Optimum Child*, for your personal sun sign and there are articles on a variety of subjects written by well-known astrologers from around the country. Much more than just a horoscope guide! Entertaining and fun the year around. New larger 5¼ x 8 format. **State year $6.95**

Llewellyn's DAILY PLANETARY GUIDE: Includes all of the major daily aspects plus their exact times in Eastern and Pacific time zones, lunar phases, signs and voids plus their times, planetary motion, a monthly ephemeris, sunrise and sunset tables, special articles on the planets, signs, aspects, a business guide, planetary hours, rulerships, and much more. Large 5¼ x 8 format for more writing space, spiral bound to lie flat, address and phone listings, time-zone conversion chart and blank horoscope chart. **State year $9.95**

To order, call 1-800-THE-MOON
Prices subject to change without notice

Llewellyn's ASTROLOGICAL CALENDAR: Large wall calendar of 48 pages. Beautiful full-color cover and full-color paintings inside. Includes special feature articles by famous astrologers, and complete introductory information on astrology. It also contains a lunar gardening guide, celestial phenomena, a blank horoscope chart, and monthly date pages which include aspects, Moon phases, signs and voids, planetary motion, an ephemeris, personal forecasts, lucky dates, planting and fishing dates, and more! 10 x 13 size. Set in Eastern time, with fold-down conversion table for other time zones worldwide. **State year $12.00**

MYTHS OF THE GODS & GODDESSES CALENDAR: Explore the mythic wilderness each month with 12 original and breathtaking paintings of figures from the archives of our collective unconscious. Meet Gods & Goddesses from a host of world cultures and find elements of your own life in their universal stories. Accompanying text explains the significance of the myth. All ancient and modern holidays are included. **State year $12.00**

Llewellyn's MAGICAL ALMANAC: This beautifully illustrated almanac explores traditional earth religions and folklore while focusing on magical myths. Each month is summarized in a two-page format with information that includes the phases of the moon, festivals and rites for the month, as well as detailed magical advice. This is an indispensable guide for anyone who is interested in planning rituals, spells and other magical advice. It features writing by some of the most prominent authors in the field. **State year $6.95**

Llewellyn's ASTROLOGICAL POCKET PLANNER: Daily Ephemeris & Aspectarian: Designed to slide easily into a purse or briefcase, this all-new annual is jam-packed with those dates and planetary information astrologers need when forecasting future events. Comes with a regular calendar section, a smaller section for projecting dates into the year ahead, a 3-year ephemeris, a listing of planetary aspects, a planetary associations chart, a time-zone chart and retrograde table. **State year $7.95**

To order, call 1-800-THE-MOON
Prices subject to change without notice

EARTH, AIR, FIRE & WATER
More Techniques of Natural Magic
Scott Cunningham

A water-smoothed stone . . . The wind . . . A candle's flame . . .
A pool of water. These are the age-old tools of natural magic.
Born of the Earth, possessing inner power, they await only our
touch and intention to bring them to life.

The four Elements are the ancient powerhouses of magic.
Using their energies, we can transform ourselves, our lives
and our worlds. Tap into the marvelous powers of the natural
world with these rites, spells and simple rituals that you can
do easily and with a minimum of equipment. Earth, Air, Fire
& Water includes more than 75 spells, rituals and ceremonies
with detailed instructions for designing your own magical
spells. This book instills a sense of wonder concerning our
planet and our lives; and promotes a natural, positive practice
that anyone can successfully perform.

0-897542-131-8, 240 pp., 6 x 9, illus., softcover   **$9.95**

PSYCHIC EMPOWERMENT FOR HEALTH AND FITNESS
Joe H. Slate, Ph.D.

Can you really "program" your mind during sleep for positive health results the next day? Yes! In fact, the ability of the mind to access the highest dimensions of reality can actually facilitate weight loss, self-control, and, ultimately, optimal fitness.

Psychic Empowerment for Health and Fitness walks you through a program of psychic exercises that actually can transform your physical body. Your upward spiral to feeling great will begin quickly with Dr. Slate's structured 7-Day Plan for Health & Fitness. You'll tap your mind's deep power and soon experience a relief from stress and anxiety. Find out why psychic protection procedures really are necessary to your health. See for yourself how psychokinesis (PK) and crystals can energize and heal our earth and all her populations. Effect an environmental clearing or a tree power interfusion. The actions you take based on this book will not only benefit you, but our planet as well.

1-56718-634-3, 256 pp., 6 x 9   **$14.95**

To order, call 1-800-THE-MOON
Prices subject to change without notice

PSYCHIC DEVELOPMENT FOR BEGINNERS
An Easy Guide to Releasing and Developing
Your Psychic Abilities
William Hewitt

Psychic Development for Beginners provides detailed instruction on developing your sixth sense, or psychic ability. Improve your sense of worth, your sense of responsibility and therefore your ability to make a difference in the world.

Benefits range from the practical to spiritual. Find a parking space anywhere, handle a difficult salesperson, choose a compatible partner, and even access different time periods! Practice psychic healing on pets or humans—and be pleasantly surprised by your results. Use psychic commands to prevent dozing while driving. Preview out-of-body travel, cosmic consciousness and other alternative realities. Instruction in Psychic Development for Beginners is supported by personal anecdotes, 44 psychic development exercises, and 28 related psychic case studies to help students gain a comprehensive understanding of the psychic realm.

1-56718-360-3, 216 pp., 5¼ x 8, softcover   **$9.95**